THE
GLORIOUS
CHURCH

WATCHMAN NEE

Living Stream Ministry
Anaheim, California • www.lsm.org

First Edition, 1968.

ISBN 0-87083-745-1

Published by

Living Stream Ministry
2431 W. La Palma Ave., Anaheim, CA 92801 U.S.A.
P. O. Box 2121, Anaheim, CA 92814 U.S.A.

Printed in the United States of America

00 01 02 03 04 05 / 14 13 12 11 10 9 8 7 6 5

CONTENTS

iii

PREFACE

The content of *The Glorious Church* in this edition differs in several respects from the first American edition published in 1968. In the process of revising *The Glorious Church* for inclusion in *The Collected Works of Watchman Nee,* Mrs. Beth Rademacher presented the Living Stream Ministry with a set of handwritten notes of the messages that formed the basis of the first edition. The appendix, "The Overcomers and God's Dispensational Moves," based on these notes, is a significant and previously unpublished portion of a message given by Watchman Nee during this conference. According to K. H. Weigh's notes, the original titles of the conference messages were as follows:

1. Introduction
2. Introduction (cont.)
3. The Relationship between God's Plan and the Church
4. The Types of the Church in God's Plan
5. The Body of Christ and the Bride of Christ
6. The Church and the Kingdom of God
7. The Relationship between the Overcomers and the Church
8. The Relationship between the Overcomers and the Kingdom
9. The Overcomers and God's Dispensational Moves
10. The Basic Qualifications and Attitude of the Overcomers
11. The Wife of the Lamb
12. The Ushering In of the Kingdom and Eternity
13. Characteristics of the Bride of Christ
14. Characteristics of the Bride of Christ (cont.)

Scripture references have been updated to reflect the contents of the Recovery Version, published by Living Stream Ministry.

The foreword that follows was originally written as a preface for the first edition of *The Glorious Church.*

FOREWORD

The following chapters are translations of a series of messages spoken in Chinese by Brother Watchman Nee to the church in Shanghai and the co-workers who were under his training for a longer period, from the fall of 1939 to the fall of 1942. These were times of spiritual revelations and heavenly visions concerning "the deep things of God." The stress was primarily on the triumphant church, the glorious Body of Christ, the full expression of Him who fills all in all. In these messages tremendous light was poured upon the four significant women in the Scriptures: Eve in Genesis 2, the wife in Ephesians 5, the woman in Revelation 12, and the Bride in Revelation 21 and 22. Their record gives us a full scope of the glorious church in God's eternal plan, the church that satisfies His desire. The span of the picture they present is so broad that it spans from eternity past through eternity future. The contents of the messages are so revealing and enlightening, so deep and profound, that they need much prayerful reading with a thorough realization and digestion in the spirit. May the Lord, the glorious Head of the Body, grant us a spirit of wisdom and revelation that we may see and apprehend the visions of the reality of the church that He has shown to the author. Our prayer goes with this book, trusting that God, the Father of our Lord Jesus Christ, "who is able to do superabundantly above all that we ask or think," would work out what is revealed in these messages, "according to the power which operates in us." "To Him be the glory in the church and in Christ Jesus unto all the generations forever and ever. Amen."

Witness Lee
Los Angeles, California, U.S.A.
June 8, 1968

CHAPTER ONE

GOD'S PLAN AND GOD'S REST

Scripture Reading: Gen. 1:26—2:3; 2:18-24; Eph. 5:22-32; Rev. 12; 21:1—22:5

Four women are mentioned in these four passages of the Scriptures. In Genesis 2 the woman is Eve; in Ephesians 5 she is the church; in Revelation 12 she is the woman seen in the vision; and in Revelation 21 she is the wife of the Lamb.

May God grant us light to see how these four women are related to one another and to His eternal plan. Then we may see the position the church occupies and the responsibility she bears in this plan and how the overcomers of God will accomplish His eternal purpose.

GOD'S PURPOSE IN CREATING MAN

Why did God create man? What was His purpose in creating man?

God has given us the answer to these questions in Genesis 1:26 and 27. These two verses are of great significance. They reveal to us that God's creation of man was indeed an exceedingly special one. Before God created man, He said, "Let us make man in our image, after our likeness: and let them have dominion over the fish of the sea, and over the fowl of the air, and over the cattle, and over all the earth, and over every creeping thing that creepeth upon the earth." This was God's plan in creating man. "God said, Let us..." This speaks of the kind of man God wanted. In other words, God was designing a "model" for the man He was to create. Verse 27 reveals God's creation of man: "So God created man in his own image, in the image of God created he him; male and female created he them." Verse 28 says, "God blessed them, and God said unto them, Be fruitful, and multiply, and replenish the earth, and subdue it: and have dominion over the fish of the sea, and over the fowl of the air, and over every living thing that moveth upon the earth."

From these verses we see the man that God desired. God desired a ruling man, a man who would rule upon this earth; then He would be satisfied.

How did God create man? He created man in His own image. God wanted a man like Himself. It is very evident then that man's position in God's creation is entirely unique, for among all of God's creatures man alone was created in God's image. The man that God's heart was set upon was completely different from all other created beings; he was a man in His own image.

We notice here something quite remarkable. Verse 26 says, "Let us make man in *our* image, after *our* likeness..."; but verse 27 says, "So God created man in *his* own image, in the image of God created he him; male and female created he them." In verse 26 the pronoun "our" is plural, but in verse 27 "his" is singular. During the conference of the Godhead, verse 26 says, "Let us make man in *our* image"; therefore, according to grammar, verse 27 should say, "So God created man in *their* own image." But strangely, verse 27 says, "So God created man in *his* own image." How can we explain this? It is because there are three in the Godhead—the Father, the Son, and the Spirit, yet only one has the image in the Godhead—the Son. When the Godhead was designing man's creation, the Bible indicates that man would be made in "our" image (since They are one, "our image" was mentioned); but when the Godhead was in the actual process of making man, the Bible says that man was made in "his" image. "His" denotes the Son. From this we ascertain that Adam was made in the image of the Lord Jesus. Adam did not precede the Lord Jesus; the Lord Jesus preceded him. When God created Adam, He created him in the image of the Lord Jesus. It is for this reason it says "in his image" rather than "in their image."

God's purpose is to gain a group of people who are like His Son. When we read Romans 8:29 we find God's purpose: "Because those whom He foreknew, He also *predestinated* to be conformed to the image of His Son, that He might be the Firstborn among many brothers." God desires to have many sons, and God desires all these sons to be like that one Son of His. Then His Son will no more be the only Begotten, but the Firstborn among many brethren. God's desire is to gain such a group of people. If we see this, we will realize the preciousness of man, and we will rejoice whenever man is mentioned. How God values man! Even He Himself became a man! God's plan is to gain man. When man is gained by God, God's plan is accomplished.

It is by man that God's plan is fulfilled, and through man His own need is met. What, then, does God require from the man whom He created? It is that man should rule. When God created man, He did not predestine man to fall. Man's fall is in chapter three of Genesis, not chapter one. In God's plan to create man, He did not predestine man to sin, neither did He foreordain redemption. We are not minimizing the importance of redemption, but only saying that redemption was not foreordained by God. If it were, then man would have to sin. God did not foreordain this. In God's plan to create man, man was ordained to rule. This is revealed to us in Genesis 1:26. Here God unveils to us His desire and tells us the secret of His plan. "Let us make man in our image, after our likeness: and let them have dominion over the fish of the sea, and over the fowl of the air, and over the cattle, and over all the earth, and over every creeping thing that creepeth upon the earth." This is God's purpose in creating man.

Perhaps some may ask why God has such a purpose. It is because an angel of light rebelled against God before man's creation and became the devil: Satan sinned and fell; the Daystar became the enemy of God (Isa. 14:12-15). God, therefore, withdrew His authority from the enemy and put it, instead, into the hand of man. The reason God created man is that man may rule in the place of Satan. What abounding grace we see in God's creation of man!

Not only does God desire that man should rule, but He marks out a specific area for man to rule. We see this in Genesis 1:26: "Let them have dominion over the fish of the sea, and over the fowl of the air, and over the cattle, and over all the earth..." "All the earth" is the domain of man's rule. Not only did God give man dominion over the fish of the sea, the birds of the heavens, and the cattle, but He further required that man should rule over "all the earth." The area where God desired man to rule is the earth. Man is especially related to the earth. Not only in His plan to create man was God's attention focused upon the earth, but after God made man, He clearly told him that he was to rule over the earth. Verses 27 and 28 say, "So God created man in his own image, in the image of God created he him; male and female created he them. And God blessed them, and God said unto them, Be fruitful, and multiply, and replenish the earth, and subdue it...." What God emphasized here is that man should "replenish the earth" and "subdue it"; it is of secondary importance that man should have dominion over the fish of the sea, the fowl of the air, and every living thing on the earth. Man's dominion over these other things is an accessory; the main subject is the earth.

Genesis 1:1-2 says, "In the beginning God created the heavens and the earth. And the earth was waste and void; and darkness was upon the face of the deep" [ASV]. These two verses are made more clear by translating them directly from the Hebrew. According to the original language, verse one says, "In the beginning God created the heavens and the earth." The heavens here are plural in number and refer to the heavens of all the stars. (The earth has its heaven, and so do all the stars.) The direct translation of verse two is: "And the earth became [not "was"] waste and void; and darkness was upon the face of the deep." In Hebrew, preceding "the earth" there is the conjunction "and." "In the beginning God created the heavens and the earth"; there were no difficulties, no problems, but then something happened: "and the earth became waste and void." The word "was" in Genesis 1:2 ("And the earth was waste and void") and the word "became" in Genesis 19:26, where Lot's wife became a pillar of salt, are the same. Lot's wife was not born a pillar of salt; she became a pillar of salt. The earth was not waste and void at the creation, but later became waste and void. God created the heavens and the earth, but "the earth became waste and void." This reveals that the problem is not with the heavens but with the earth.

We see then that the earth is the center of all problems. God contends for the earth. The Lord Jesus taught us to pray, "Your name be sanctified; Your kingdom come; Your will be done, as in heaven, so also on *earth*" (Matt. 6:9-10). According to the meaning of the original language, the phrase "as in heaven, so also on earth" is common to all three clauses, not only to the last clause. In other words, the original meaning is: "Your name be sanctified, as in heaven, so also on earth. Your kingdom come, as in heaven, so also on earth. Your will be done, as in heaven, so also on earth." This prayer reveals that there is no problem with "heaven"; the problem is with the "earth." After the fall of man, God spoke to the serpent, "Upon thy belly shalt thou go, and dust shalt thou eat all the days of thy life" (Gen. 3:14). This meant that the earth would be the serpent's sphere, the place upon which he would creep. The realm of Satan's work is not heaven, but earth. If the kingdom of God is to come, then Satan must be cast out. If God's will is to be done, it must be done on earth. If God's name is to be sanctified, it must be sanctified on earth. All the problems are on the earth.

Two words in Genesis are very meaningful. One is "subdue" in Genesis 1:28, which can also be translated "conquer." The other is "keep" in Genesis 2:15, which can also be translated "guard." We see from these verses that God ordained man to conquer and guard the earth. God's original intention was to give the earth to man as a place to dwell. It was not His intention that the earth would become desolate (Isa. 45:18). God desired, through man, to not allow Satan to intrude upon the earth, but the problem was that Satan was on earth and intended to do a work of destruction upon it. Therefore, God wanted man to restore the earth from Satan's hand.

Another matter we need to note is that God required man, strictly speaking, not only to take back the earth, but also the heaven which is related to the earth. In the Scripture there is a difference between "heavens" and "heaven." The "heavens" are where the throne of God is found, where God can exercise His authority, while "heaven" in the Scriptures sometimes refers to the heaven which is related to the earth. It is this heaven which God also wants to recover (see Rev. 12:7-10).

Some may ask: Why doesn't God Himself cast Satan into the bottomless pit or the lake of fire? Our answer is: God can do it, but He does not want to do it Himself. We do not know why He will not do it Himself, but we do know how He is going to do it. God wants to use man to deal with His enemy, and He created man for this purpose. God wants the creature to deal with the creature. He wants His creature *man* to deal with His fallen creature *Satan* in order to bring the earth back to God. The man whom He created is being used by Him for this purpose.

Let us read Genesis 1:26 again: "And God said, Let us make man in our image, after our likeness: and let them have dominion over the fish of the sea, and over the fowl of the air, and over the cattle, and over all the earth...." It seems that the sentence is finished here, but another phrase is added: "...and over every creeping thing that creepeth upon the earth." Here we see that the creeping things occupy a very great position, for God spoke of it after He finished mentioning "all the earth." The implication is that in order for man to have dominion over all the earth, the creeping things must not be overlooked, for God's enemy is embodied in the creeping things. The serpent in Genesis 3 and the scorpions in Luke 10 are creeping things. Not only is there the serpent, representing Satan, but also scorpions, representing the sinful and unclean evil spirits. The domain of both the serpent and the scorpion is this earth. The problem is on the earth.

Therefore, we must distinguish the difference between the work of saving souls and the work of God. Many times the work of saving souls is not necessarily the work of God. Saving souls solves the problem of man, but the work of God requires that man exercise authority to have dominion over all things created by Him. God needs an authority in His creation, and He has chosen man to be that authority.

If we were here just for ourselves as mere men, then all our seeking and longing would be to love the Lord more and to be more holy, more zealous, and save more souls. All of these pursuits are good indeed, but they are too man-centered. These things are concerned simply with the benefit of man; God's work and God's need are entirely neglected. We must see that God has His need. We are on this earth not merely for man's need but even more for God's need. Thank God that He has committed the ministry of reconciliation to us, but even if we have saved all the souls in the whole world, we have not yet accomplished God's work or satisfied God's requirement. Here is something called God's work, God's need. When God created man, He spoke of what He needed. He revealed His need to have man rule and reign over all His creation and proclaim His triumph. Ruling for God is not a small thing; it is a great matter. God needs men whom He can trust and who will not fail Him. This is God's work, and this is what God desires to obtain.

We do not lightly esteem the work of gospel preaching, but if all our work is just preaching the gospel and saving souls, we are not causing Satan to suffer fatal loss. If man has not restored the earth from the hand of Satan, he has not yet achieved God's purpose in creating him. Saving souls is often only for the welfare of man, but dealing with Satan is for the benefit of God. Saving souls solves man's need, but dealing with Satan satisfies God's need.

Brothers and sisters, this requires us to pay a price. We know how the demons can speak. A demon once said, "Jesus I know of, and with Paul I am acquainted; but who are you?" (Acts 19:15). When a demon meets us, will he flee or not? Preaching the gospel demands that we pay a price, but a much greater price must be paid to deal with Satan.

This is not a matter of a message or a teaching. This requires our practice, and the price is extremely great. If we are to be men whom God will use to overthrow all of Satan's work and authority, we must obey the Lord completely and absolutely! In doing other work it matters less if we preserve ourselves a little, but when dealing with Satan, we cannot leave one bit of ground for ourselves. We may hold on to something of ourselves in our study of the Scriptures, in preaching the gospel, in helping the church or the brothers, but when we are dealing with Satan, self must be utterly abandoned. Satan will never be moved by us if self is preserved. May God open our eyes to see that His purpose demands that we be wholly and absolutely for Him. A double-minded person can never deal with Satan. May God speak this word to our hearts.

THE UNCHANGEABLE PURPOSE OF GOD

God wanted to have man to rule for Him on this earth, but man did not attain to God's purpose. In Genesis 3 the fall took place and sin entered; man came under the power of Satan, and everything seemed to come to an end. Satan was seemingly victorious and God was seemingly defeated. In addition to the passage in Genesis 1, there are two more passages in the Scriptures which are related to this problem. They are Psalm 8 and Hebrews 2.

Psalm 8

Psalm 8 shows that God's purpose and plan have never changed. After the fall, God's will and requirement for man remained the same without any alteration. His will in Genesis 1, when He created man, still holds good, even though man has sinned and fallen. Even though Psalm 8 was written after man's fall, the psalmist was able to praise; his eyes were still set upon Genesis 1. The Holy Spirit did not forget Genesis 1, the Son did not forget Genesis 1, nor did God Himself forget Genesis 1.

Let us see the content of this psalm. Verse 1 says, "O Jehovah our Lord, / How excellent is Your name / In all the earth." All who are inspired by the Holy Spirit will utter such words: "How excellent is Your name in all the earth!" Though some people slander and reject the Lord's name, yet the psalmist loudly proclaimed, "O Jehovah our Lord, / How excellent is Your name / In all the earth." He did not say, "Your name is very excellent." "Very excellent" does not have the same meaning as "how excellent." "Very excellent" means that I, the psalmist, can still describe the excellence, whereas "how excellent" means that even though I can write psalms, I do not have the words to express, nor do I know how excellent is the Lord's name. So I can only say, "O Jehovah our Lord, how excellent is Your name in all the earth!" Not only is His name excellent, His name is excellent "in all the earth"! The expression "in all the earth" is the same as in Genesis 1:26. If we know God's plan, every time we read the word "man" or the word "earth" our hearts should leap within us.

Verse 2 continues, "Out of the mouths of babes and sucklings / You have established strength / Because of Your adversaries, / To stop the enemy and the avenger." Babes and sucklings refer to man, and the emphasis in this verse is upon God using man to deal with the enemy. The Lord Jesus quoted this verse in Matthew 21:16: "Out of the mouth of infants and sucklings You have perfected praise." These words mean that the enemy may do all he can, but it is not necessary for God Himself to deal with him. God will use babes and sucklings to deal with him. What can babes and sucklings do? It says, "Out of the mouths of babes and sucklings / You have established strength." God's desire is to obtain men who are able to praise; those who can praise are those who can deal with the enemy.

In verses 3 through 8 the psalmist says, "When I see Your heavens, the works of Your fingers, / The moon and the stars, which You have ordained, / What is man, that You remember him, / And the son of man, that You visit him? / You have made him somewhat lower than angels / And have crowned him with glory and honor. / For You have caused him to rule over the works of Your hands; / You have put all things under his feet: / All sheep and oxen, / As well as the beasts of the field, / The birds of heaven and the fish of the sea, / Whatever passes through the paths of the seas." If we were writing this psalm, perhaps we would add a parentheses at this point: "How pitiful that man has fallen and sinned and been cast out of the garden of Eden! No more can man attain to this." But thank God, in the heart of the psalmist there was not such a thought. In God's view the earth can still be restored, the position given to man by God still exists, and His commitment to man to destroy the work of the devil still remains. Therefore, starting from the third verse, the psalmist again narrates the same old story, completely ignoring the third chapter of Genesis. This is the outstanding feature of Psalm 8. God's purpose is for man to rule. Is man worthy? Certainly not! But since God's purpose is for man to rule, man will surely rule.

In verse 9 the psalmist again says, "O Jehovah our Lord, / How excellent is Your name / In all the earth!" He continues to praise, as though he were not even aware of man's fall. Though Adam had sinned and Eve had also sinned, they could never withstand God's plan. Man can fall and man can sin, but man cannot overthrow the will of God. Even after man fell, God's will toward man remained the same. God still requires man to overthrow the power of Satan. Oh, what an unchangeable God He is! His way is unswerving and utterly straightforward. We must realize that God can never be overthrown. In this world there are some who receive many hard blows, but no one has been attacked daily and received continual blasts like God. Yet His will has never been overthrown. What God was before man's fall, He is after man's fall and after sin entered into the world. The decision He affirmed aforetime is still His decision today. He has never changed.

Hebrews 2

Genesis 1 speaks of the will of God at creation, Psalm 8 speaks of God's will after man's fall, and Hebrews 2 speaks of God's will in redemption. Let us look at Hebrews 2. We will see that in the victory of redemption God still desires man to obtain authority and deal with Satan.

In verses 5 through 8a the writer says, "For it was not to angels that He subjected the coming inhabited earth, concerning which we speak. But one has solemnly testified somewhere, saying, 'What is man, that You bring him to mind? Or the son of man, that You care for him? You have made Him a little inferior to the angels; You have crowned Him with glory and honor and have set Him over the works of Your hands; You have subjected all things under His feet [quoted from Psalm 8].' For in subjecting all things to Him,

He left nothing unsubject to Him." All things must be subject to man; God purposed it from the beginning.

But it has not yet turned out in this way. The writer continues, "But now we do not yet see all things subjected to Him, but we see Jesus, who was made a little inferior to the angels because of the suffering of death, crowned with glory and honor" (vv. 8b-9a). Jesus is the person who fits this situation. Psalm 8 said that God made man a little lower than the angels, but the apostle changed the word "man" into "Jesus." He explained that "man" refers to Jesus; it was Jesus who became a little lower than the angels. Man's redemption is by Him. God originally purposed that man should be a little lower than the angels and that man should be crowned and rule over all His creation. He intended for man to exercise authority on His behalf to cast out His enemy from the earth and from the heaven related to the earth. He wanted man to destroy all of Satan's power. But man fell and did not take his place to rule. Therefore, the Lord Jesus came and took upon Him a body of flesh and blood. He became the "last Adam" (1 Cor. 15:45).

The last part of verse 9 says, "So that by the grace of God He might taste death on behalf of everything." The birth of the Lord Jesus, the human living of the Lord Jesus, as well as the redemption of the Lord Jesus show us that His redemptive work is not only for man, but for all created things. All creation (except the angels) is included. The Lord Jesus stood in two positions: to God He was the man at the beginning, the man whom God appointed from the very first, and to man He is the Savior. In the beginning God assigned man to rule and overthrow Satan. The Lord Jesus is that man, and that man is now enthroned! Hallelujah! Such a man has overthrown the power of Satan. He is the man whom God is after and desires to obtain. In His other aspect, He is a man related to us; He is our Savior, the One who has dealt with the problem of sin in our place. We sinned and fell, and God made Him to be the propitiation for us. Furthermore, He not only became the propitiation for us, but He was also judged for all creatures. This is proved by the splitting of the veil in the holy place. Hebrews 10 tells us that the veil in the holy place signified the body of the Lord Jesus. Upon the veil were embroidered cherubim, which represent created things. At the time of the Lord's death, the veil was split in two from the top to the bottom; as a result, the cherubim embroidered upon it were simultaneously rent. This reveals that the death of the Lord Jesus included judgment for all creatures. He not only tasted death for every man, but also for "everything."

Verse 10 continues, "For it was fitting for Him, for whom are all things and through whom are all things, in leading many sons into glory." All things are for Him and through Him; all things are to Him and by Him. To be for Him means to be to Him; to be through Him means to be by Him. Praise God, He has not changed His purpose in creation! What God ordained at creation He continued to ordain after man's fall. In redemption His purpose remains the same. God did not change His purpose because of man's fall. Praise God, He is bringing many sons into glory! He is glorifying many sons. God purposed to gain a group of new men who have the likeness and the image of His Son. Since the Lord Jesus is the representative man, the rest will be like whatever He is, and they will enter with Him into glory.

How is this to be accomplished? Verse 11 says, "For both He who sanctifies and those who are being sanctified are all of One." Who is He that sanctifies? It is the Lord Jesus. Who are those that are being sanctified? We are the ones. We can read the verse in this way: "For both Jesus who sanctifies and we who are sanctified are all of One." The Lord Jesus and we are all begotten of the same Father; we have all originated from the same source and have the same life. We have the same indwelling Spirit and the same God, who is our Lord and our Father. "For which cause He is not ashamed to call them brothers." The word "He" refers to our Lord Jesus, and "them" to us. "He is not ashamed to call them brothers" because He is of the Father and we also are of the Father.

We are God's many sons, which will ultimately result in God bringing us into glory. Redemption did not change God's purpose; on the contrary, it fulfilled the purpose that was not accomplished in creation. God's original purpose was that

man should rule, especially over the earth, but man regret-
tably failed. Yet all things did not come to an end because of
the first man's fall. What God did not obtain from the first
man, Adam, He will obtain from the second man, Christ.
There was the eventful birth in Bethlehem because God ordained man to rule and restore the earth and because God
determined that the creature man should destroy the
creature Satan. This is why the Lord Jesus came to become a
man. He did it purposely, and He became a true man. The
first man did not accomplish God's purpose; rather, he
sinned and fell. He not only failed to restore the earth, but
he was captured by Satan. He not only failed to rule, but he
was brought into subjection to Satan's power. Genesis 2 says
that man was made of dust, and Genesis 3 points out that
dust was the food of the serpent. This means that fallen man
became the food of Satan. Man could no longer deal with
Satan; he was finished. What could be done? Did this mean
that God could never achieve His eternal purpose, that He
could no longer obtain what He was after? Did it mean that
God could never restore the earth? No! He sent His Son to
become a man. The Lord Jesus is truly God, but He is also
truly man.

In the whole world there is at least one man who chooses
God, a person who can say, "The ruler of the world is coming,
and in Me he has nothing" (John 14:30). In other words, in the
Lord Jesus there is not a trace of the prince of this world. We
must note carefully that the Lord Jesus came to this world
not to be God but to be man. God required a man. If God Himself dealt with Satan, it would be very easy; Satan would fall
in a moment. But God would not do it Himself. He wanted
man to deal with Satan; He intended that the creature would
deal with the creature. When the Lord Jesus became a man,
He suffered temptation as a man and passed through all the
experiences of man. This man conquered; this man was victorious. He ascended to heaven and sat down at the right hand
of God. Jesus has been "crowned with glory and honor" (Heb.
2:9). He has been glorified.

He did not come to receive glory as God, but to obtain
glory as man. We do not mean that He did not have the glory

of God, but Hebrews 2 does not refer to the glory which He possessed as God. It refers to Jesus, who was made a little lower than the angels because of the suffering of death; Jesus was crowned with glory and honor. Our Lord ascended as a man. Today He is in the heavens as man. A man is at God's right hand. In the future there will be many men who will be there. Today a man is sitting on the throne. One day there will be many men sitting on the throne. This is certain.

When the Lord Jesus was resurrected, He imparted His life into us. When we believe in Him, we receive His life. We all become God's sons, and as such, we all belong to God. Because we have this life within us, as men we can be entrusted by God to fulfill His purpose. Therefore, it says that He will bring many sons into glory. To rule is to be glorified, and to be glorified is to rule. When the many sons have obtained authority and restored the earth, then they will be brought triumphantly into glory.

We should never presume that God's purpose is merely to save us from hell that we may enjoy the blessings of heaven. We must remember that God intends for man to follow His Son in the exercise of His authority on the earth. God wants to accomplish something, but He will not do it Himself; He wants us to do it. When we have done it, then God will have attained His purpose. God desires to obtain a group of men who will do His work here on this earth, that God may rule on earth through man.

THE RELATIONSHIP
BETWEEN REDEMPTION AND CREATION

We need to note the relationship between redemption and creation. We should by no means consider that the Bible speaks of nothing but redemption. Thank God that in addition to redemption there is also creation. The desire of God's heart is expressed in creation. God's goal, God's plan, and God's predetermined will are all made known in His creation. Creation reveals God's eternal purpose; it shows us what God is truly after.

The place of redemption cannot be higher than that of creation. What is redemption? Redemption recovers what

God did not obtain through creation. Redemption does not bring anything new to us; it only restores to us what is already ours. God through redemption achieves His purpose in creation. To redeem means to restore and recover; to create means to determine and initiate. Redemption is something afterward, so that God's purpose in creation may be fulfilled. Oh, that the Lord's children would not despise creation, thinking that redemption is everything. Redemption is related to us; it benefits us by saving us and bringing us eternal life. But creation is related to God and God's work. Our relationship with redemption is for the benefit of man, while our relationship with creation is for the economy of God. May God do a new thing on this earth, so that man will not only stress the gospel but go beyond that to take care of God's work, God's affairs, and God's plan. In fact, our preaching of the gospel should be with a view to bringing the earth back to God. We must show Christ's triumph over the kingdom of Satan. If we are not Christians, that is something else. But once we have become Christians, we should not only receive the benefit of redemption but also achieve God's purpose in creation. Without redemption we could never be related to God. But once we have been saved, we need to offer ourselves to God to attain the goal for which He first made man. If we pay attention only to the gospel, that is only half of the matter. God requires the other half, that man may rule for Him upon the earth and not allow Satan to remain here any longer. This half is also required of the church. Hebrews 2 shows us that redemption is not only for the forgiveness of sins, that man may be saved, but also to restore man back to the purpose of creation.

Redemption is comparable to the valley between two peaks. As one descends from one peak and proceeds to ascend the other, he encounters redemption at the lowest part of the valley. To redeem simply means to prevent man from falling any further and to uplift him. On the one hand, God's will is eternal and straightforward, without any dip, so that the purpose of creation may be achieved. On the other hand, something happened. Man has fallen, and man has departed from God. The distance between him and God's eternal

purpose has become farther and farther apart. God's will
from eternity to eternity is a straight line, but ever since his
fall, man has not been able to attain to it. Thank God, there
is a remedy called redemption. When redemption came, man
did not need to go down anymore. After redemption man is
changed and begins to ascend. As man continues to rise the
day will come when he will again touch the one straight line.
The day that line is reached is the day the kingdom will
come.

We thank God that we have redemption. Apart from it
we would plunge lower and lower; we would be suppressed
by Satan more and more until there would be no way to rise.
Praise God, redemption has caused us to return to God's
eternal purpose. What God did not obtain in creation and
what man lost in the fall are completely regained in redemption.

We must ask God to open our eyes to see what He has done
so that our living and work may have a real turn. If all our
work is just to save others, we are still a failure, and we
cannot satisfy God's heart. Both redemption and creation are
for the obtaining of glory and the overthrowing of all the
power of the devil. Let us proclaim the love of God and the
authority of God as we see the sin and the fall of man. But at
the same time, we must exercise spiritual authority to overthrow the devil's power. The commission of the church is
twofold: to testify the salvation of Christ and to testify the
triumph of Christ. On the one hand, the church is to bring
benefit to man, and on the other hand, it is to cause Satan to
suffer loss.

GOD'S REST

In all six days of God's work of creation, His creation of
man was distinct. All His work throughout the six days was
for this. His real aim was to create man. In order to do this,
God first had to repair the ruined earth and heaven. (Genesis
2:4 says, "These are the generations of the heavens and of the
earth when they were created, in the day that the Lord God
made the earth and the heavens." "The heavens and the
earth" refer to the creation in the beginning, since at that

time it was the heavens that were first formed and then the earth. But the second part, "in the day that the Lord God made the earth and the heavens," refers to His repair and restoration work, since in this work the earth was cared for first and then the heaven.) After God restored the ruined earth and heaven, He created the man of His design. After the sixth day, there was the seventh day; on this day God rested from all His work.

Rest comes after work: work must be first, and then rest may follow. Moreover, work must be completed to entire satisfaction before there can be any rest. If the work has not been done completely and satisfactorily, there can never be any rest to the mind or heart. We should not, therefore, esteem lightly the fact that God rested after six days of creation. For God to rest is a great matter. It was necessary for Him to have gained a certain objective before He could rest. How great the power must be which moved such a Creator God to rest! To cause such a God, who plans so much and who is full of life, to enter into rest requires the greatest strength.

Genesis 2 shows us that God rested on the seventh day. How is it that God could rest? The end of Genesis 1 records that it was because "God saw every thing that he had made, and, behold, it was very good" (v. 31).

God rested on the seventh day. Before the seventh day, He had work to do, and prior to His work, He had a purpose. Romans 11 speaks of the mind of the Lord and His judgments and ways. Ephesians 1 speaks of the mystery of His will, His good pleasure, and His foreordained purpose. Ephesians 3 also speaks of His foreordained purpose. From these Scriptures we gather that God is not only a God who works, but a God who purposes and plans. When He delighted to work, He proceeded to work; He worked because He wished to work. When He found satisfaction with His work, He rested. If we desire to know God's will, His plan, His good pleasure, and His purpose, we have only to look at that which caused Him to rest. If we see that God rests in a certain thing, then we may know that is something He was originally after. Man too cannot rest in that which does not satisfy him; he must gain what he is after and then he will have rest. We must not regard this rest lightly, for its meaning is very great. God did not rest in the first six days, but He rested in the seventh day. His rest reveals that God accomplished His heart's desire. He did something which made Him rejoice. Therefore, He could rest.

We must note the word "behold" in Genesis 1:31. What is its meaning? When we have purchased a certain object with which we are particularly satisfied, we turn it around with pleasure and look it over well. This is what it means to behold. God did not just casually "look" upon all that He had made and see that it was good. Rather, He "beheld" everything which He had made and saw that it was very good. We need to take note that God was there at the creation "beholding" what He had made. The word "rested" is the declaration that God was satisfied, that God delighted in what He had done; it proclaims that God's purpose was attained and His good pleasure was accomplished to the fullest. His work was perfected to such an extent that it could not have been made better.

For this reason God commanded the Israelites to observe the Sabbath throughout their generations. God was after something. God was seeking something to satisfy Himself, and He attained it; therefore, He rested. This is the meaning of the Sabbath. It is not that man should purchase fewer things or walk less miles. The Sabbath tells us that God had a heart's desire, a requirement to satisfy Himself, and a work had to be done to fulfill His heart's desire and demand. Since God has obtained what He was after, He is at rest. It is not a matter of a particular day. The Sabbath tells us that God has fulfilled His plan, attained His goal, and satisfied His heart. God is One who demands satisfaction, and He is also One who can be satisfied. After God has what He desires, He rests.

What then brought rest to God? What was it that gave Him such satisfaction? During the six days of creation there were light, air, grass, herbs, and trees; there were the sun, the moon, and the stars; there were fish, birds, cattle, creeping things, and beasts. But in all these God did not find rest. Finally there was man, and God rested from all His work. All of the creation before man was preparatory. All of God's expectations were focused upon man. When God gained a man, He was satisfied and He rested.

Let us read Genesis 1:27-28 again: "So God created man in his own image, in the image of God created he him; male and female created he them. And God blessed them, and God said unto them, Be fruitful, and multiply, and replenish the earth, and subdue it: and have dominion over the fish of the sea, and over the fowl of the air, and over every living thing that moveth upon the earth." Now read Genesis 1:31 with Genesis 2:3: "And God saw every thing that he had made, and, behold, it was very good....And God blessed the seventh day, and sanctified it: because that in it he had rested from all his work which God created and made." God had a purpose, and this purpose was to gain man—man with authority to rule over the earth. Only the realization of this purpose could satisfy God's heart. If this could be obtained, all would be well. On the sixth day God's purpose was achieved. "God saw every thing that he had made, and, behold, it was very good...and he rested on the seventh day from all his work." God's purpose and expectation were attained; He could stop and rest. God's rest was based upon man who would rule.

CHAPTER TWO

THE TYPE OF EVE

In creation two persons were created: one was Adam and the other was Eve. Both were created human beings, but each typify something different. First Corinthians 15 says that Adam was a type of the Lord Jesus, and Romans 5 says that Adam was a figure of the man who was to come. Adam, then, foreshadowed Christ; he portrayed Christ in figure. In other words, all that God purposed in Adam was to be achieved in Christ.

But besides Adam in the creation, there was also the woman, Eve. God very carefully recorded the creation of this woman in Genesis 2, and when we come to Ephesians 5 we are clearly told that Eve typifies the church. Therefore, we can see that God's eternal will is achieved partly through Christ and partly through the church. In order for us to understand how the church can achieve God's will on earth, we must learn from Eve. The purpose of this book is not to discuss the type of Adam. Therefore, we will not consider this matter here; rather, the emphasis is upon Eve. We are not focusing our thoughts upon the work of Christ, but upon the position the church occupies in relation to that work.

When we read Genesis 2:18-24 and Ephesians 5:22-32 we find that a woman is mentioned in both places. In Genesis 2 there is a woman, and in Ephesians 5 there is also a woman. The first woman is a sign typifying the church; the second woman is the first woman. The first woman was planned by God before the foundation of the world and appeared before the fall. The second woman was also planned before the foundation of the world, but was revealed after the fall. Although one appeared before the fall and the other after, there is no difference in God's sight: the church is the Eve of Genesis 2. God created Adam to typify Christ; God also created Eve to typify the church. God's purpose is not only accomplished by Christ but is also accomplished by the church. In Genesis 2:18, the Lord God said, "It is not good that the man should be alone; I will make him a help meet for him." God's purpose in creating the church is that she may be the help meet of Christ. Christ alone is only half; there must be another half, which is the church. God said, "It is not good that the man should be alone." This means that in God's sight Christ alone is not good enough. Genesis 2:18-24 reiterates the events of the sixth day of creation. On the sixth day God created Adam, but afterward it seems that He considered a little and said, "No, it is not good that the man should be alone." Therefore, He created Eve for Adam. By then, everything was completed, and we find that Genesis 1 ends with this record: "And God saw every thing that He had made, and, behold, it was very good" (v. 31). From this we realize that having Adam alone, or we may say, having Christ alone, is not enough to satisfy God's heart. With God there must also be Eve, that is, there must also be the church. Then His heart will be satisfied.

The Lord God said, "It is not good that the man should be alone." In other words, God desired to have both Adam *and* Eve. His purpose is to have a victorious Christ plus a victorious church, a Christ who has overcome the work of the devil plus a church which has overthrown the work of the devil. His purpose is to have a ruling Christ and a ruling church. This is what God planned for His own pleasure, and He has performed it for His own satisfaction. It has been done because God desired to do it. God desired to have Christ, and God also desired to have a church which is exactly like Christ. God not only desired that Christ would have dominion, He also wants the church to have dominion. God allows the devil on earth because He said, "Let them," Christ and the church, "have dominion." God purposed that the church, as Christ's counterpart, should take part in dealing with Satan. If the church does not match Christ, God's purpose will not be fulfilled. In warfare Christ needs a help meet, and even in glory He also needs a help meet. God requires the church to be the same as Christ in every respect. It is God's desire that Christ should have a help meet.

EVE CAME OUT OF ADAM

Adam needed a help meet. What did God do to meet this need? Genesis 2:19-20 says, "And out of the ground the Lord God formed every beast of the field, and every fowl of the air; and brought them unto Adam to see what he would call them: and whatsoever Adam called every living creature, that was the name thereof. And Adam gave names to all cattle, and to the fowl of the air, and to every beast of the field; but for Adam there was not found a help meet for him." God brought every kind of living creature before Adam, but Adam could not find his help meet among them. None of the living creatures made out of earth could be a help meet for Adam.

Therefore, "the Lord God caused a deep sleep to fall upon Adam, and he slept; and he took one of his ribs, and closed up the flesh instead thereof. And the rib, which the Lord God had taken from man, made he a woman, and brought her unto the man. And Adam said, This is now bone of my bones, and flesh of my flesh: she shall be called Woman, because she was taken out of Man" (vv. 21-23). This one was Adam's help meet and the figure of the church in Ephesians 5. The Bible says very clearly that all of the things made of earth and not taken out of the body of Adam could not be his help meet. All the beasts of the field, the cattle, and the birds of the air were made of earth. They were not taken out of Adam; therefore, they could not be the help meet to Adam. We must remember that Eve was formed out of a rib taken from Adam; therefore, Eve was the constituent of Adam. This means that the church comes out of Christ. Only that which is out of Christ can be the church. Anything that is not of Christ is not the church.

We need to note a few more words in Genesis 1:26 and 27. Verse 26 says, "And God said, Let us make man in our image, after our likeness: and let *them*...." In the Hebrew language the word "man" is singular, but immediately following, the plural pronoun "them" is used. The same pattern is used in verse 27 which says, "So God created man in his own image, in the image of God created he him; male and female created he them." The noun "man" is singular, but the following pronoun "them" is plural. God created one man; but we can also say that He created two! One is two, and yet the two are one because Eve was *in* Adam.

Notice further that verse 27 says, "God created man in his own image, in the image of God created he him; male and female created he them." The way God created "man" is the *same way* He created "them." Not only was Adam created, but Eve also was included in him. "God created *man* in his own image." This "man" is singular and typifies Christ. "In the image of God created He...them." "Them" is plural and typifies Christ and the church. God not only wants to have an only begotten Son, He also wants many sons. The many sons must be just like the one Son. From these verses we see that if the church is not in a state which corresponds with Christ, God will not rest and His work will not be completed. Not only is Adam in the image of God, so also is Eve. Not only does Christ have the life of God, the church also has God's life.

THE CHURCH COMES OUT OF CHRIST

We should then ask, "What is the church?" The church is that part which is taken out of Christ. We need to see the two aspects of Adam, and then it will be easy for us to understand. On one hand, Adam stands merely as himself; on the other hand, he is a type. As far as Adam himself is concerned, he was made of clay. All natural men are made of clay. But Adam also typified Christ. The fact that Eve was made from Adam signifies that the church is made from Christ. Eve was made with Adam's rib. Since Eve came out *from* Adam, she was still Adam. Then what is the church? The church is another form of Christ, just as Eve was another form of Adam.

The church is just Christ. Oh, there are many people who think that the church is the coming together of the "people" who believe in the Lord and who are saved. No, this is not true! Then who constitutes the church? The church is only that portion which has been taken out of Christ. In other words, it is the man which God has made by using Christ as the material. It is not a man made of clay. The material of the church is Christ. Without Christ, the church has no position, no life, no living, and no existence. The church comes out of Christ.

First Corinthians 10:17 says, "Seeing that there is one bread, we who are many are one Body." This verse means that even though we are many, the bread which we break is one; therefore, the Body is also one. The apostle Paul clearly stated that the one loaf represents the Body of Christ, that is, the church as a whole. Though we are many, yet the Body is one. When we remember the Lord, I take a little piece from the loaf, you take a little piece from the loaf, and others do the same. For many centuries throughout the world, all Christians have taken a little portion of this loaf and eaten it! If you could take all the pieces they have eaten and put them together, they would become the whole church. The church is not an individual "I" plus an individual "you." It is not Mr. Smith plus Mr. Jones or even all the Christians in the whole world put together. The church is the Christ in you, the Christ in him, and the Christ in all the Christians around the world throughout all the centuries put together. Our natural man has nothing to do with the church. The only part of us which is related to the church is the portion of the loaf which we have eaten. This is especially shown in the Gospel of John, where it is revealed that all those who believe in the Lord have Christ dwelling in them and are therefore one in the Spirit.

The church is composed of that which is out of Christ. Man's talent, ability, thought, strength, and all that he has are outside the church. Everything that comes from the natural life is outside the church, and anything that is brought into the church of the natural life will only result in a tearing down, not a building up. Only that which comes out of Christ is in the church. Eve was not made from clay, but from Adam, the one who typified Christ. The preciousness is that God took a rib from Adam and made Eve. Only that which came out from Adam, not from clay, can be called "Eve," and only that which comes from Christ can be called the church. Whatever is not from Christ has nothing to do with the church.

Some people were very frank before they believed in the Lord. After they were saved, they used their frankness to serve God. They considered their natural frankness to be quite useful; they were proud of it. But from what source does their frankness come? Is it from Christ? Has it been dealt with by the cross? Oh, if it is not out of Christ, if it has never been dealt with by the cross, it is of no use to the church! Eve was constituted only of that which came out of Adam, and the church, likewise, is constituted only of that which is out of Christ. Whatever is of man himself is not the church.

Some people were very eloquent before they believed. It was so easy for them to narrate and describe something to others. After they are saved, they just change the subject matter and begin to preach. But we should not consider it sufficient that such people can preach well. Rather, we should ask, "From what source does their eloquence come? Has it been dealt with by the cross?" If their eloquence is that which they originally had and has never been dealt with by the cross, then it is entirely from their own nature. The eloquence which they bring into the church will be something of the earthly Adam. The church will actually be pulled down by these people. Only that which comes out of Christ is the church; nothing which comes out of human nature is the church.

We may also meet some people who are very clever. Their minds are exceptionally keen. Before they were saved, they used their mind to study philosophy, science, and literature. After they are saved, they simply use their mind to study God's Word. But we must ask, "From where does this keen mind come? Has it been dealt with by the cross? Is it under the control of the Holy Spirit? Or is it just that mind which they had originally?" If this is so, it is simply something out of the earthly Adam, out of the man himself, the human nature; it is something of the flesh. Although these people have changed the subject, their mind is still the same old mind! And when they use this mind to study the Bible, instead of helping the church, they will cause the church to suffer loss. Only that which is out of Christ can be the church. Whatever is of man is not the church.

God must deal with us to such a degree that everything from our human nature will be brought under control. Our natural strength must be dealt with by the cross and subjected to the rule of the Holy Spirit. Only then will we not cause the church to suffer loss. Everything which issues from the natural, Adamic life within us is made of earth and not wanted by God. Only that which was made of Adam's rib was Eve. (The bone refers to the resurrection life. When the Lord was on the cross, not one of His bones was broken.) Only that which is formed from the resurrection life of Christ is the church.

Eve must be made of the bone of Adam. Without the bone from Adam, there would have been no Eve. Adam's help meet is also Adam's body, since the source of Eve's life was his very bone. Adam was the basis of her existence. She could exist only because a part of Adam was in her. It is the same with the church. We need to continually declare to the Lord, "We owe everything to You. Without You we have no life, no existence, nothing! We come out of You!"

The vital issue of our new birth is just this: Repentance does not make us a part of the church; neither does our confession of sins nor our faith. Only the life which Christ has imparted to us makes us a part of the church. The basis of our being a part of the church is our new birth, since it is then that Christ imparts Himself to us. Therefore, there is a need for us to live, behave, and act according to this life, the life of Christ. God cannot do anything more for us than to impart His Son into us that we may share the life of Christ. Even though we are just earthen vessels, there is a great treasure within us. What then can shake us? However, if we act according to ourselves, we are outside the church. Anything other than the portion of Christ in us is not the church; it is simply our own selves. If we work according to ourselves, we are not doing the Lord's work. We must ask ourselves upon what basis and from what source we are serving the Lord, doing His work, pursuing spiritual things, and leading a spiritual walk. Is everything we do based upon Christ or based upon ourselves? If we do everything by Christ, we can accomplish God's purpose, but if we do anything by ourselves, even though something is accomplished, it can only be of an earthly nature and cannot accomplish God's eternal will.

God's eternal purpose is to gain a man. This man is a corporate man coming out of Christ. It is the church. The church is not a matter of several Christians being put together with several other Christians. It is not so many "men"; it is a *life.* The church is the church only because there are many people who all share the same life, the same Christ. You have a portion of Christ, and he has a portion of Christ; each one of us has a portion of Christ. When all of these portions of Christ are put together, there is the church.

We must be clear that God does not want individuals. God created man, male and female. The male is singular, and the female is also singular. Christ is singular, and the church is also singular. In the sight of God there is only one Christ and only one church. In the future we will see that there is only one man in Hades and only one man in the heavens; there is no third man. In God's eyes, He only sees two men in the whole world. First Corinthians 15 reveals that Adam is the first man and Christ is the last man. There are no others. The Body of Christ, just as Eve, is one—not many!

Therefore, even though we have God's life within us, we still need God to work upon us to break our individualism. God must break down the thought that I myself am enough. We need to be one with all the rest of God's children. There is only one Eve; likewise, there is only one Body of Christ. All of God's children, all who share the life of Christ, are not many individual men and women; they are all one man. God must break our individualism. He must crush us day after day until we come to know the life of the Body.

There are many who think that they can be Christians all by themselves! But God will not allow this. Often their individual prayers are not answered, their personal study of the Scriptures does not enlighten them, and their individual seeking does not lead them to God's will. If such a person would say to another brother or sister, "I just cannot get through this matter by myself, would you help me?", and they prayed together, he would be clear eventually. Whatever he could not understand by himself, he would see clearly when an answer was sought with his brother. Such a person is often still proud, thinking that he can make it by himself most of the time, and that there are only a few times when he cannot get through. This is individualism. In the church individualism must be broken. We must allow the Christ in us and the Christ in all the other brothers and sisters to become knit together in one Body.

Many Christians know the life we have in Christ, but we must regretfully say, they do not know the life in the Body of Christ. Just as the life of Christ is a reality, the life of the Body of Christ is also a reality. Christians are not individuals; they are one. The apostle Paul said that though we are many, we are still *one* bread and *one* Body. If we live according to Christ, we are one with all other Christians. But if we live according to ourselves, we separate ourselves from all of God's children.

Therefore, if the church is to become a real church, two steps are necessary: the spreading or increase of Christ and the consuming of our self. The spreading of Christ began when we were regenerated, and since we were saved, the Lord has been working on us day after day to consume our self. The Lord will continue to work until one day before God, we say, "There is not a single thing I can do by myself. Everything I do is done according to the principle of mutual help among the members. All that I do is according to the principle of fellowship, which is the principle of the Body." The church is the Body of Christ. Only that which is of Christ is the church; whatever issues from man is not.

We must realize that God takes into account the source of things, not whether they are good or evil. Men always ask, "Is this good or bad?" But God asks, "Where does it come from?" That which came from Adam was called Eve; likewise, that which comes from Christ is called the church. Anything which is not out of Christ is not the church. Men ask, "Do you have love?" But God asks, "Where does your love come from?" Men ask, "Are you zealous?" But God asks, "What is the source of your zeal?" We need to solve the matter of origin, not good or evil. The question of good and evil came in after Genesis 3. Perhaps someone would say, "Do I not have some ability? Am I not zealous?" But the problem is, where does your ability and zeal come from?

We often feel that we are quite able to love and help others by ourselves. To love and help others, of course, is good, but "if I deliver up my body that I may boast, but do not have love," Christ's love, "I profit nothing" (1 Cor. 13:3). Is it wrong to give ourselves to help others? The issue is still: Where does it come from? Only that which comes from Christ is the church. Anything that is not out of Christ has nothing to do with the church.

In our Christian life, the first lesson and last lesson we need to learn is to discern the source of things. The first lesson is to reject anything that comes from ourselves, and the last lesson is still to reject anything that comes from our-selves. This does not mean that we should not strive or be zealous, but the issue is that our striving and zeal must come from the Lord. We are not saying that we should not work, but we want work which is initiated by the Lord. We are not saying that we should not seek after power, but that we should seek the power which is from the Lord. This is the whole issue: From where does it originate?

In the Gospel of John, the Lord Jesus once said, "The Son can do nothing from Himself" (John 5:19). According to the Greek text, the word "from" can also be translated "out of." This means that the Son can do nothing out of Himself. If this was the case with the Lord, then how much more it should be with us! How can we ever do anything from ourselves? We need to see before God that we can do nothing from ourselves. He must bring us to the place where we realize that we truly can do nothing from ourselves—everything must be by Him and out of Him.

When we serve the Lord, it is not enough to be zealous. No, we must do that work which the Lord assigns to us. In Colossians 1:29, Paul said, "For which also I labor, struggling according to His operation which operates in me in power."

God is working within us so we can work without. We often do many things outwardly, but not much has been done inwardly. God has not done that much within; most everything has been done by ourselves. This kind of work, even though it may be considerable, is of no use. In the matter of serving the Lord, God must bring us to a place that we do not want anything that is not from the Lord. If the Lord is not moving, then we will not dare move.

Eve was bone of Adam's bone and flesh of his flesh. This signifies that the bones inside and the flesh outside are all out of Christ. Everything on the inside and everything on the outside are of Him; nothing can be from ourselves. Everything of Eve was out of Adam, and everything of the church is out of Christ. No matter how well we may do something, it is absolutely useless in achieving God's eternal purpose. No matter how good something is, it cannot possibly glorify God if it issues from ourselves.

The first woman represents the woman who is after God's heart. There was not only a man who expressed God's heart, there was also a woman. It is not only Christ who satisfies God's heart; it is also the church. Christ satisfies God's heart, because He allows God to be His head. It must be the same with the church. She also must allow God to be her head. When the church reaches this position, the will of God will be done. God intends to have this kind of people on the earth, and when He does, His heart's desire will be satisfied. Let us remember that whatever comes out from man's self is just dust and not worthy of being the material for the help meet. Only that which comes out from Christ is the church.

EVE MADE FROM ADAM'S SLEEP—
THE CHURCH PRODUCED THROUGH CHRIST'S
"NON-REDEMPTIVE DEATH"

We have already seen that Eve was not made of dust, but of Adam; Adam was the material of which Eve was made. Likewise, Christ is the material for the church. God used Christ to make the church. Now we will see how Eve was made, and how the church was made.

Let us read Genesis 2:21-23. "And the Lord God caused a deep sleep to fall upon Adam, and he slept; and he took one of his ribs, and closed up the flesh instead thereof. And the rib, which the Lord God had taken from man, made he a woman, and brought her unto the man. And Adam said, This is now bone of my bones, and flesh of my flesh: she shall be called Woman, because she was taken out of Man."

God brought forth the church out of the death of Christ. Regarding the death of Christ, the words in Genesis 2 are very special. It says, "The Lord God caused a deep sleep to fall upon Adam" (v. 21). This verse does not say that God caused Adam to die, but that He caused him to fall into a deep sleep. If death had been mentioned, then sin would be involved, because verse 17 in the preceding passage says that death and sin are related. Adam's sleep typifies the aspect of Christ's death which was not related to redemption. In the death of Christ there was an aspect which was not related to redemption but to the release of Himself. We are not saying that the death of Christ is not for redemption—we truly believe that it is—but His death involved an aspect which is not related to redemption. This aspect is the releasing of Himself for the creation of the church. It has nothing to do with sin. God is taking something out of Christ and using it to create the church. Therefore, "sleep" is used to typify His death through which man receives life.

Redemption and the receiving of life are two distinct things. Redemption involves a negative aspect of dealing with our sins. We have sinned and deserve to die; therefore, Christ came to bear our sins. His death accomplished redemption for us. This aspect of His death is related to sin. But there is another aspect of His death which is not related to redemption: It is the imparting of Himself to us so that through His death we may receive life.

Adam's sleep was not for Eve's redemption; it was so that a rib could be taken out for her creation. (Sin had not yet entered the scene—that account is in Genesis 3.) Eve came into existence through Adam. Eve was able to receive life because Adam slept. In the same manner, an aspect of the death of Christ is for the imparting of life to the church.

When Adam fell into a deep sleep, God took a rib from him. Likewise, when Christ died, something happened to His rib, His side (see John 19:31-37). His side was not pierced for redemption, because the piercing occurred *after* His death. The problem of redemption had already been solved. According to Jewish custom, whoever was crucified had to be taken away before sunset. If they were not dead, the soldiers would break their bones to speed their death. The two thieves who were crucified with the Lord had not died; therefore, their bones were broken. But when the soldiers looked at the Lord Jesus and saw that He was already dead, they did not break His bones. Instead, they pierced His side with a spear, and blood and water flowed out. This signifies that when His side was pierced, the work of redemption had already been accomplished. It reveals that the work of Christ not only involved the shedding of His blood to redeem us from sins, but also the flowing out of water, typifying the imparting of His life to us. This aspect is apart from sin and redemption. The blood deals with our sins, while the water causes us to receive His life. This is what His wounded side speaks to us.

We all need to clearly distinguish these two aspects of Christ's death. One is for redemption, while the other is not for redemption. The first aspect of His death deals with all that happened after man's fall in Genesis 3. Since man fell, Christ came to redeem us in order to bring us back to the original purpose of God's creation of man. But the other aspect of His death has nothing to do with sins. It is entirely for the releasing of His life, that His life may be imparted into us.

Because of these two distinct aspects in the death of Christ, the Bible uses two different substances to typify them. Blood is used for redemption; water is used for the non-redemptive aspect. May God open our eyes to see the importance of this matter. The blood is for redemption, and the water is for the imparting of His life. Because we have committed sins and are sinful before God, the blood is ever before Him, speaking for our sins. But the water typifies the Lord Himself as life. John 19:34 says that the water flowed out from Him, and in chapter twenty, the Lord pointed out His side to His disciples. John 20 is not a chapter dealing with redemption. The Lord said, "I ascend to My Father and your Father, and My God and your God" (v. 17). This is a matter of imparting life.

This is not all. Let us read Genesis 2:22 and 23 again: "And the rib, which the Lord God had taken from man, made he a woman, and brought her unto the man. And Adam said, This is now bone of my bones, and flesh of my flesh." In one place in the Scriptures, we are referred to as "flesh and blood" (1 Cor. 15:50), but when the Scriptures refer to man in resurrection, he is described only as "flesh and bones"; there is no mention of blood (see Luke 24:39). God used Adam's rib to make Eve; He did not use Adam's blood. Throughout the whole Bible, the word *blood* is mentioned more than four hundred times, but in Genesis 2 there is no mention of blood because the matter of redemption was not at issue. Whenever blood is mentioned, redemption is involved. Blood is for redemption. The Old Testament records how man used the blood of beasts for atonement of sins. In the New Testament, Hebrews 9:22 says, "Without shedding of blood there is no forgiveness." Whether in the Old Testament or the New Testament, we see that blood is related to redemption. But in the creation of Eve, blood was not mentioned because there was no sin; God saw no sin there.

THE CHURCH IN GOD'S PLAN—WITHOUT SIN

When we read Ephesians 5:25, we find the same meaning. "Husbands, love your wives even as Christ also loved the church and gave Himself up for her." In this passage we need to notice three points:

First, Christ gave Himself up for us because we are the church. Romans 5, which speaks of Christ dying for sinners, is in reference to redemption. Ephesians 5, however, does not deal with the problem of sinners but with the issue of the church. The context of Ephesians 5 is not that Christ came to die for us because we were sinners, but that He gave Himself up for us because we are the church.

Second, Christ gave Himself for us because He loves us, not because we have sinned. According to 1 Corinthians 15, Christ died for our sins, but Ephesians 5 says that Christ loved the church and gave Himself for it. He gave Himself because of love, not because of our sin. To die for sin is one thing, but to die for love is entirely different. To die for sin deals with the problem of sin—this is redemption. But Christ's giving Himself for us is a matter of love. Sin is not involved in Ephesians 5. This aspect of His death is related to love and has nothing to do with sin.

Third, Christ gave Himself for us in order to give Himself *to* us, without any question of our sins. This verse may be translated, "Christ also loved the church and gave Himself *to* the church." Adam imparted his bone to Eve; Christ has imparted Himself to us as well. We have Him within us because He died; He has already entered into us. Because He died, we now have His very life within us. He Himself has been imparted to us.

Let us consider this for a moment. Is this not wonderful? From God's point of view, the church has never sinned and has never been related to sin. It is true that God knew that man fell and needed to be redeemed, but marvelously, along another line, He did not see sin at all. In other words, there is a portion in us which has no need of redemption. This is the portion which we have received from Christ. It does not need to be redeemed because it transcends sin. (We obtained this portion, of course, after we were redeemed.) This portion is the church.

The Scriptures reveal how God has used many women to typify the church. Genesis contains, in addition to the story of Eve, the story of Rebecca and Asenath. Rebecca's marriage to Isaac typifies the church being offered to Christ. Asenath's marriage to Joseph and her bearing sons in Egypt typifies the church being chosen out of the world unto God. Exodus speaks of Zipporah being married to Moses in the wilderness. This typifies the church in the wilderness. Joshua speaks of Achsah, who after being married, asked for the upper springs and the lower springs. This typifies the church receiving the inheritance. Ruth's marriage to Boaz typifies the redemption of the church. Abigail's marriage to David typifies the church enlisted as an army for warfare.

The Old Testament speaks of many women who typified the various aspects of the church; the church was chosen from the world, redeemed, taken through the wilderness, enlisted for warfare, given the inheritance, and offered to Christ. All of these types in the Scriptures refer to the church, but of them all, the type in Genesis 2 is unique. There is no other type similar to it because Eve portrays the church as it really is in God's mind and the place it has in His eternal plan. All the other types occur after man's fall; only the type of Eve precedes the fall. All the other types involve the matter of moral responsibility; this one alone is free of it.

The Eve that God made came out of Adam, not out of a redeemed sinner. She was made before sin occurred. In like manner, the church comes out of Christ; it is not a matter of sinners receiving grace and being saved. Eve came out of Adam and was wholly for Adam; even so, the church comes out of Christ and is wholly for Christ.

We may consider that the church is composed of many people who have been saved—people like Ruth. Ruth was totally involved in sin, and Boaz came to redeem her. But this is not the picture of the church which Genesis 2 gives to us. By the time of Ruth sin had already entered, but in Genesis 2 there was no problem of sin. This is the church which was in the beginning; it had no association with sin. Oh, this is a tremendous matter, and these are very meaningful words. The church in God's forethought has no history of sin!

When people inquire concerning the history of our salvation, we always start with the fall, that is, how we committed sin and wandered in sin, how we were so evil and bad, and how we heard the gospel, believed on the Lord Jesus, and were saved. We always start with the fall. But in God's eyes, the church has never been touched by sin. The church is the part out of Christ which has never been touched by sin and known sin. That which is completely without sin is called Eve, and that which is wholly out of Christ is called the church. That which is entirely from Christ and will be solely for Christ is Eve, the church. Eve typifies a corporate man made by God—the church that is wholly of Christ. The church is not a composition of human beings from every nation, race, and people. No! Only that which comes out of Christ can be called the church. It is not that many people believe in Jesus and become the church. The church is the portion which is out of Christ alone. We must see that the church is the vessel chosen by God to manifest His Son, Christ, and to achieve His eternal purpose. It has nothing to do with sin and has never touched sin.

We must have our thoughts renewed and enter into the matter which God considers the greatest. Many of God's children refer everything to the problem of sin and being saved. They are always thinking about how they were so sinful and how they were saved. It seems that we are always looking from the perspective of sin. This matter is always with us, but God intends to turn our thinking completely around. He wants us to have an entirely new view of the church; He wants us to see that she is not related to sin at all. From beginning to end, the church is out of God and for God and has never touched sin. There is a portion in us which is out of Christ and which is Christ Himself. This portion has never been and never can be related to sin; sin has no way to come into contact with it. We can truly say that there is something in us which is holy. Oh, may we all enter into God's view of the church! From His viewpoint it appears that He has canceled all history of sin.

When we give our praises to Him in eternity, it will not be necessary for us to mention what kind of sinners we have been. God desires to bring us to a stage that all of the history succeeding Genesis 3 will pass away and only that which is of Christ will be brought to Him. This is God's eternal purpose! God desires to obtain a church, a corporate man, in whom everything is out of Christ and for Christ, a church in which there is no history of sin.

Let us turn back to Genesis 2:18. "And the Lord God said, It is not good that the man should be alone; I will make him a help meet for him." The creation of Eve was for the satisfaction of God's heart's desire. Because He had such a desire, He performed it. We must note that the creation of Eve is recorded in Genesis 2, before the events in Genesis 3 came to pass. There was no problem of moral responsibility between God and man because sin had not yet entered. Man had no problem with God; therefore, all the events recorded in Genesis 2 were for the purpose of meeting the needs of God Himself, not to deal with the shortcomings of man. God's creation of Eve in Genesis 2 shows how God purposed to have His church from eternity to eternity. The first thing in the sight of God was not man's fall but the plan which He purposed in eternity past. God's plan in eternity was for man to exercise His authority and spoil all the work of Satan. This is God's purpose for the church, and it will all be fulfilled in the coming eternity. God is after such a church to satisfy His heart. After He made male and female, He entered into rest. God was satisfied because He obtained such a church.

CHAPTER THREE

THE BODY OF CHRIST
AND THE BRIDE OF CHRIST

We have already seen how Eve typifies the church in God's plan. In God's plan all that is of the church is completely out of Christ. It contains nothing of man and has no relationship with sin. Our God is determined to have such a church. Anything less than this can never satisfy His heart. He not only planned this kind of church, but He is going to obtain it. Hallelujah! It is a fact! We must realize that our God can never be hindered or frustrated. When He purposes something, even though Hades and all of creation's forces would rise to oppose Him, He cannot be resisted. Even though we are fallen and full of failure, even though we are fleshly and soulish, departing far from God and disobeying Him, God will still attain His purpose. No matter what man does, he cannot ruin God's plan; the most he can do is delay it. Therefore, we must not only realize God's purpose, but also be clear that God will fully attain what He has purposed. From eternity God purposed to obtain a church completely out of Christ, a church containing no impurity of man, no element of earth, nor any savor of sin. Every part of her is something out of Christ, and Christ is her very life.

Beginning with Genesis 3, however, man fell. Now we not only have the fact of God's purpose in creation, but also the fact of man's fall. Therefore, let us see the way that God devised to amend the situation.

Ephesians 5:25-30 says, "Husbands, love your wives even as Christ also loved the church and gave Himself up for her that He might sanctify her, cleansing her by the washing of the water in the word, that He might present the church to

Himself glorious, not having spot or wrinkle or any such things, but that she would be holy and without blemish. In the same way the husbands also ought to love their own wives as their own bodies; he who loves his own wife loves himself. For no one ever hated his own flesh, but nourishes and cherishes it, even as Christ also the church, because we are members of His Body."

These six verses of Scripture may be divided into two sections: verses 25-27 tell us the first reason husbands should love their wives; verses 28-30 tell us the second reason husbands should love their wives. In these two sections we see two commands to love the wife and we see two reasons. But there is a difference between these two sections. The first section says that Christ "loved" the church and "gave" Himself up for her—these verbs are in the past tense. Beginning with verse 28, the verbs are in the present tense, such as "nourishes" and "cherishes." These two portions of Scripture, therefore, involve different elements of time—one section refers to something in the past and the other to the present.

The subjects of these two sections are also different. The first section refers to the church as the *bride* of Christ; the second section speaks of the church as the *Body* of Christ. In the first section, the past tense is used when the church is referred to as the bride of Christ. This is because the whole purpose of Christ, as revealed to us, is to have a bride. Even His death was for the purpose of obtaining a bride. Although He will obtain His bride in the future, the work was finished in the past. Concerning the present, the church is the Body of Christ, and the Lord is presently nourishing and cherishing His church.

THE RELATIONSHIP
BETWEEN THE BODY AND THE BRIDE

In the Lord's eyes, the church has two positions: as to her life, the church is the Body of Christ, but regarding her future, she is the bride of Christ. As to the union of Christ with the church, the church is His Body; regarding the intimate relationship of Christ with the church, the church is His bride.

Whenever God's Word speaks of the oneness between Christ and the church, we see Christ as the Head and the church as His Body. Whenever the Word shows the distinction between Christ and the church, we see the church as the bride to Christ. Adam and Eve were spoken of as two becoming "one flesh," but they were still two persons; God still counted them as two. Adam was Adam, and Eve was Eve. They were united to be one. This is the relationship between the church and Christ. From one they became two, and from two they became one. When God first created man, He made male and female. Eve came out from Adam; thus, she and Adam were one. Even so, the church comes out from Christ; therefore, the church and Christ are also one. However, since Adam and Eve both existed at the same time, there was a distinction between them. Likewise, since the church and Christ coexist, there is also a distinction between them. Regarding oneness, they are one, but as to the matter of distinction, they differ from each other.

These two positions have to do with a difference in time. Today the church is the Body of Christ, but in the future the church will be the bride of Christ. Today the church is the Body of Christ for the purpose of manifesting the life of Christ. One day, when the church is mature in life, God will bring the church to Christ; in that day she will become the bride of Christ. Some people think that the church is the bride of Christ today, but this is wrong. There is no such thing. Since the Lord Jesus is not yet the Bridegroom, how could the church already be His bride? God will not bring the church to Christ as His bride until the work of the church as the Body of Christ has been accomplished.

If we look at the type in Genesis 2, we can also see the relationship between the Body and the bride. Eve was made out of Adam's rib, so she was the body of Adam. Since a portion of Adam's body was used to make Eve, her position was the body of Adam. But after Eve was made, God brought her to Adam, and she became the bride of Adam. This is the relationship between the Body and the bride. When reference is made to Eve coming out of Adam, it means that she is the body of Adam; but when Eve was brought to Adam and became his help meet; she became Adam's bride. That which was out of Adam was the body of Adam, and that which was brought to Adam was his bride.

Only that which came out of Adam could become the help meet of Adam. Whatever was not out of Adam could never be his help meet. Thus, when all the birds of the air were brought to him, Adam did not take any of them as his help meet, for they were not out of him. When all the cattle were brought to him, Adam did not take any of them, because they also were not out of him. It was the same with all the beasts. Their origin was not right. Since they were not out of Adam, they could not be his help meet. Who then could be the help meet of Adam? Eve could! Eve was brought to Adam just as the birds of the air, the cattle of the field, and the beasts were brought. However, there was a basic difference between Eve and them; they were not out of Adam. Since Eve was the only one who came out from Adam, she alone was qualified to be his bride. Coming out from him, she was brought back to him. Whatever comes out from him is his body; whatever is brought back to him is his bride.

Only that which comes out of Christ can return to Christ. That which does not come out from Christ can never return to Him. Only that which comes from heaven can return to heaven. If we have not come down from heaven, we will not be able to return to heaven. Home is the place of our origin. When we say that we are going home, we mean that we are returning to the place from which we have come. Only that which is from heaven can return to heaven. Only that which was from Adam could return to Adam. Adam could receive only that which was out of himself. This was a type—showing that Christ will receive only that which is out of Himself. Only those who come out from Christ can return to Him. Only those who receive life from Him can be received by Him.

There are many people who feel that they should offer all that they are and all that they have for the Lord's use. But God cannot accept anything which is offered from a human source. God cannot take or use anything which comes out from man himself. Among all Christians, especially among those who are quite zealous, a serious mistake is often made.

They think that everything will be fine as long as they offer themselves, their abilities, their talents, and all they have to the Lord. But we must remember that Christ will accept only that which comes out of Himself; He will not accept anything which comes out of man.

You may say, "Among the apostles, was there not a Paul? Was he not well educated? Was he not a man of great intelligence?" But we must remember the words that Paul spoke about himself. "For I did not determine to know anything among you except Jesus Christ, and this One crucified. And I was with you in weakness and in fear and in much trembling; and my speech and my proclamation were not in persuasive words of wisdom but in demonstration of the Spirit and of power" (1 Cor. 2:2-4). We thank God that intelligent and eloquent men can come into the church, but their natural, original intelligence and their natural, original eloquence are of no spiritual use in the church. In the church only one thing is recognized—that which comes out of Christ. Only that which is out of Christ can return to Christ. The material for the building of such a bride is Christ Himself.

The matter we need to attend to is this: only that which is out of Christ can be of any value and spiritual use in the church. God never uses the old creation to construct the new creation. Neither does God use that which is of man to construct that which is of God. He can never, never use fleshly things to produce something spiritual. The Lord Jesus said, "That which is born of the Spirit is spirit" (John 3:6b). Would it be possible for that which is born of the flesh to become spirit? No! "That which is born of the flesh is flesh." All problems issue from the matter of source. If we want to know whether the result will be spiritual, we need only ask whether the source is spiritual. The Lord Jesus said, "That which is born of the Spirit is spirit." We cannot use anything of the flesh to produce something of the spirit. A message which issues from thoughts only produces thoughts. Work done by stirring up the emotion only produces emotional stimulation. Only work from the spirit produces the spirit. The question is not whether the goal or the purpose is right, but what the process is. Man considers that as long as the goal is right, everything else is right. But God not only asks if the goal is right, He also asks how we do it. Someone may say, "I am for the Lord, and the work I am doing is for the church—the work of saving souls, spiritual work, the work of extending the heavenly kingdom. I have given all my ability and intelligence to it. Isn't this good?" In spite of this, man's natural ability and intelligence—that which has not been dealt with by the cross—are of no spiritual use. The Lord said, "That which is born of the flesh is flesh" (v. 6a).

Thus, it is not only necessary to have a spiritual purpose, but the process must also be of the spirit. The method must be of the spirit, and the man himself must be one who is of the spirit. Only that which is from the Holy Spirit can be spiritual. Only that which was out of Adam could return to Adam. First it must be Adam's body, and then it could be Adam's bride. First we must be the Body of Christ, and then we can be brought back to be the Bride of Christ. We hope that we may touch some spiritual reality in this matter. We need to see what God is really after. He requires that everything be out of Christ, that everyone be born of the Spirit.

Every Christian, therefore, must pursue the life of the Body. If we do not seek the life of the Body, we cannot seek the life of the Bride. We should never think that it does not matter much whether we experience the life of the Body. We must realize that if we have the life of the Body today, we will have the life of the Bride in the future. If we live vaguely and aimlessly today, we will never know the life of the bride. Every Christian must know the Body of Christ. In the sight of God, we must seek after this. We cannot just live as individuals; we must walk together with other children of God. A Christian must see that he is a member of the whole Body. He is not simply one Christian among many, but he is also a member. He must live as a member with many other Christians, having a mutual, Body-relatedness with them. If we really know the life of the Body, we will see that a Christian cannot live one day without the Lord Jesus, and neither can he live one day without other Christians. Without the Lord Jesus he cannot exist, and without other Christians he cannot exist. God is after a Body, not many single, isolated Christians. God desires a whole Eve, not a hand here and a foot there. He must obtain Eve as a whole being; then she will be of use to Him. He does not want one who is disabled. He wants a new man, a corporate man.

For this reason all division and individualism must be eliminated. The matter of division is not merely something outward—it is a problem of our heart. Martin Luther said that the greatest pope does not live in Rome but right in our hearts. We must realize that the greatest hindrance to God's will is not outward divisions but ourselves, as individual persons, who do not know the life of the Body. At this point we need two different revelations: first, to see that the Body is one, and second, to see that we are part of it, that we are members of this Body. When we see that the Body is one, we will never dare to be divisive. When we see that as members we are but a portion of the whole Body, we will never dare to justify ourselves, or consider that, as single members, we could be a whole unit. Only the whole Body together can be a unit. We ourselves as members are too small, too insufficient. Oh, may God deliver us from being individualists. Then we may become those who are useful to Him.

CHRIST LOVES THE CHURCH

Now let us read Ephesians 5:28-29. "In the same way the husbands also ought to love their own wives as their own bodies; he who loves his own wife loves himself. For no one ever hated his own flesh, but nourishes and cherishes it, even as Christ also the church." Husbands should love their wives, because loving their wives is loving their own bodies. Men always nourish and cherish their own bodies, and Christ also nourishes and cherishes the church. In the eyes of Christ, the church is His own Body, bone of His bone and flesh of His flesh. These verses show us that the church is the Body of Christ, and that His work toward the church today is to nourish and cherish it, because the church is Himself. He certainly will nourish and cherish us, because we all have come out of Christ. We know how well we nourish and cherish ourselves. In the same way, Christ will nourish and cherish us.

It is a fact that "no one ever hated his own flesh." If a normal person hurts his hand, he carefully cherishes his hand; if his foot is injured, he tenderly cares for it. Men always nourish and cherish themselves. Similarly, Christ loves the church, because the church is His very self.

Let us read Ephesians 5:25-27. "Husbands, love your wives even as Christ also loved the church and gave Himself up for her that He might sanctify her, cleansing her by the washing of the water in the word, that He might present the church to Himself glorious, not having spot or wrinkle or any such things, but that she would be holy and without blemish." These three verses speak of the church as the Bride of Christ. "That He might present the church to Himself" presents a scene of God bringing Eve to Adam. In like manner Christ will bring the church and present it to Himself. This presenting, however, is in the future. The church today has not yet attained to this place. Christ is working step by step in the church until that day when He presents her to Himself. In other words, Ephesians 5:25-27 speaks of the path from redemption to the kingdom. Step by step the church is now being prepared so that Christ may present it to Himself in that day.

Why does it say here that the church must be "cleansed"? It is because this is Ephesians 5, not Genesis 2. God's highest revelation of the church is seen in the book of Ephesians. The outstanding feature of this book is that it does not start with sinners being saved but with our having been chosen in eternity. Romans 1 speaks first of sin—how we sinned and then were saved. But Ephesians 1 starts from eternity and our being chosen before the foundation of the world. The problem of sin is not mentioned until chapter two. The book of Ephesians reveals two lines: one is from eternity to eternity, and the other is from man's fall to his redemption. In Ephesians something transcendent is revealed to us. We see how the church comes out from Christ, how it was chosen before the foundation of the world, and how it will forever manifest the glory of Christ in eternity. At the same time, it shows us that man's fall is a fact, that man's committing of sin is a fact, and that the existence of our natural life is also a fact. Therefore, chapter five says that Christ will cleanse us by the washing of water in the word until we are sanctified. He wants to restore us to the point that we completely match God's eternal will.

On the one hand, we need the vision to see that the church has never failed, sinned, or fallen. The church has never touched sin; from eternity to eternity she has been on a straight line. On the other hand, we need to see that we are just a group of sinners saved by grace; therefore, we need the washing of the water in the word. We need His life, by means of His word, to sanctify us and restore us to the highest point. May God grant us grace so that we may reach that point.

THE CLEANSING OF THE CHURCH
BY THE WASHING OF THE WATER IN THE WORD

We must notice this phrase "by the washing of the water in the word." In the New Testament two Greek words are used to denote *word*. One is *logos*, referring to the word in a general sense; the other is *rhema*, which although translated as *word* in Scripture, means something quite different from *logos*. *Logos* refers both to things which have been eternally determined and to things used in an objective way. This is *word*, as we generally use it, and *word*, as it is generally known in Christianity. But *rhema* refers to words which are spoken. This is more subjective than *logos*. Let us look at several passages in the New Testament where *rhema* is used.

In Matthew 4:4 Jesus said, "It is written, 'Man shall not live on bread alone, but on every word that proceeds out through the mouth of God.'" In this verse "word" is *rhema*, not *logos*. When we say that the Bible is the Word of God, the "word" is *logos*, not *rhema*. Can we say that man shall not live by bread alone, but by the Word of God recorded in the Bible? No. We are not saying that the written Word of God is of no use, but that *logos*—the Word of God recorded in the Bible—is of no use to us *by itself*. One day a messenger came to tell a mother that her son had been run over by a car and was at the point of death. The mother immediately opened the Bible and happened to turn to John 11:4: "This sickness is not unto death...." Because of this verse she felt peaceful and even began to rejoice, but when she arrived at the scene of the accident, she found that her son had already died. Did this mean that what is recorded in the Gospel of John is not the Word of God? It is the Word of God, but it is *logos,* not *rhema.* The word she grasped was not the word which God spoke to her at that specific instance. Both *logos* and *rhema* are the Word of God, but the former is God's Word objectively recorded in the Bible, while the latter is the word of God spoken to us at a specific occasion.

Romans 10:17 says, "So faith comes out of hearing, and hearing through the word of Christ." In this verse *rhema,* not *logos,* is again used. This means that we can believe when Christ first speaks within us.

John 3:16 is a verse many of us can quote from memory. Perhaps we have known it for ten or twenty years. Is this verse the Word of God? Certainly it is the Word of God, but it is *logos.* There comes a day, however, when we read this verse and it is entirely different to us than it ever was before. "For God so loved the world...." Now, God does not just love the world, He loves me. "...that He gave His only begotten Son..." God did not give His Son just to the world, but to me. "...that every one who believes into Him..." It is not that someone believes into Him, but that I believe into Him. "...would not perish, but would have eternal life." It is I who will not perish, and it is I who even now have eternal life. This word is now *rhema.* God speaks the word to us, and at the same moment, we have faith. Therefore, we must ask God, "O God, if You would be gracious to me, I pray that You would always give me *rhema.*" This does not mean that *logos* is of no use. *Logos* has its definite use, for without *logos,* we could never have *rhema.* All the *rhema* of God is based upon *logos.* We cannot deny that John 3:16 is the Word of God. But when the *logos* of God becomes the *rhema* spoken by God to us, we have faith and the whole matter is settled.

John 6:63 says, "The words which I have spoken to you are spirit and are life." Did the Jews not have the *logos* of God? Yes, they did. They were very familiar with it and could recite the Old Testament commandments very well, but it was of no use to them. Only the words which the Lord spoke to them were spirit and life. Only *rhema* is spirit and life.

Mark 14:72 says, "And immediately a rooster crowed a second time. And Peter remembered the word, how Jesus had said to him, Before a rooster crows twice, you will deny Me three times. And thinking upon it, he wept." Peter recalled the *rhema* that Jesus had spoken to him. The *rhema* was that which was brought to his remembrance. While Peter was telling a lie, suddenly *rhema* came. The very sentence of the Lord came to him. *Rhema* is the word which the Lord has spoken, and now He speaks it again.

In Luke 1:38 Mary said, "Behold, the slave of the Lord. May it happen to me according to your word. And the angel departed from her." In this verse *rhema* is used. This was not just a word of prophecy in Isaiah 7:14, "Behold, the virgin will conceive and will bear a son," but a word that was spoken specifically to Mary by the angel, "Behold, you will conceive in your womb and bear a son" (Luke 1:31). Because Mary heard this, she received strength and it was accomplished.

In Luke 2:29 Simeon said, "Now You release Your slave, Master, according to Your word, in peace." "Word" in this verse is *rhema*. Before the Lord Jesus came, God spoke His word to Simeon that he would not see death until he had seen the Lord's Christ. But on the day he saw the Lord Jesus, Simeon said, "Now You release Your slave, Master, according to Your word, in peace." Simeon had *rhema* from the Lord. It was not according to a certain chapter or a certain verse in the Bible, but it was according to the word spoken to him on that day by the Lord. Merely having the word from a certain chapter and verse in the Bible is not sufficient. Only the word which the Lord speaks to us is of any use. The *rhema* reveals something to us personally and directly; it shows us what we need to deal with and what we need to be cleansed from. We must specifically seek after this very matter, because our Christian life is based on this *rhema*. What word has God really spoken to us, and how has He spoken to us? We must remember that today's Christianity is still the Christianity of personal revelation. If the Lord does not speak within man, it is not Christianity, nor is it the New Testament.

Luke 3:2 says, "During the high priesthood of Annas and Caiaphas, the word of God came to John the son of Zachariah in the wilderness." "Word" in this verse is also *rhema*.

Luke 5:5 says, "Simon answered and said, Master, through the whole night we toiled and caught nothing; but based on Your word I will let down the nets." The "word" in this verse was something spoken by the Lord for that occasion. It was the Lord speaking personally to Simon. This is *rhema*. The Lord did not speak in a certain chapter and verse of the Scripture that Simon should let down the net. If someone attempted to walk on the sea because of Matthew 14:29, he would certainly sink. This is not the word which the Lord is speaking today, though He did speak it on that day. It is true that the word spoken by God in the past and the word He speaks today carry the same authority; they have never changed. But the important thing is this: Is God speaking that very word to us today?

Luke 24:8 says, "They remembered His words (*rhema*)." In short what is *rhema*? *Rhema* is something the Lord has spoken previously which He is now speaking again. In other words, *rhema* is the word which the Lord speaks the second time. This is something living.

In Acts 11:16 Peter said, "And I remembered the word of the Lord, how He said, John baptized in water, but you shall be baptized in the Holy Spirit." While Peter was preaching to the household of Cornelius, the Spirit of the Lord fell upon them, and the word of the Lord came to Peter. It was not that Peter tried to recall the word from his memory, but it was the Lord who spoke to him, "John baptized with water, but you shall be baptized in the Holy Spirit."

We will always treasure the fact that the Lord still speaks today. He not only spoke in the Scriptures, He not only spoke to Paul and John, He is also speaking to us today. The word of the Lord has never ceased. Whenever someone who is working for the Lord stands up to speak for Him, he must expect the *rhema*. If the Lord does not speak to us today, we are really failures. How many times have we preached, yet the Lord did not speak a word? It is not that there was something wrong with the message, but it was all the general word of the Lord; there was no *rhema* in it. The problem with the church today is that it lacks the living word of the Lord; instead there are only dead doctrines. There is a real shortage of direct communication from God. There is only a passing on of man's preaching. It is pitiful that so many people have died under good doctrines! May God have mercy upon us and give us *rhema*. May He speak personally and directly to us today. Only when we have *rhema* can we move ahead and have the living water to supply to others. What we need is *rhema*.

In the eternal plan of God the church is without sin. The church has no history of sin; it is entirely spiritual and wholly out of Christ. But what about the actual history of the church? We know that she has not been completely out of Christ, and much of her element has been of the earth. In what way will Christ bring the church into perfection? He will do it by cleansing her with the washing of the water in the word—the *rhema*. We have mentioned previously that water refers to life. It typifies the life that was released through the non-redemptive aspect[1] of the death of Christ. Christ is using His life in His word, His *rhema*, to cleanse us.

What is the meaning of Christ cleansing us by His life through His word? First, we must see the church's problem from God's viewpoint. Her defect is not that the Christ whom she has received is too little, but that she has too many things other than C hrist. The church in God's will comes entirely out of Christ, without any sin, without any flesh, and containing no natural life. But what about our actual condition? Every one of us who truly belongs to Christ has a certain portion which is solely and wholly Christ. We thank God for this portion. In addition to this portion, we still have many things which are not of Christ. We need to be cleansed because of all these other things. What is the meaning of

[1]The two aspects of the death of Christ are: (1) dealing with all the negative things, and (2) preparation for all the positive things—all the things in the life of Christ. Thus the life which was released thrugh His death is not for redemption. Redemption is the negative aspect of the death of Christ.

cleansing? It means to subtract, not to add. If cleansing meant an addition to us, then it would be a dyeing. Eve in Genesis 2 did not need to be cleansed, because she typified the church in God's eternal plan. But if we consider that we do not need to be cleansed today, we are deceiving ourselves. God plans to bring us to the place where cleansing is not necessary, but today we still need to be cleansed.

How does God cleanse us? He does it with His life through His own word. Many times we do not know in which aspect we need to be cleansed. But one day the life within us will not let us go. Before long His *rhema* comes into us, indicating what must be dealt with. On the one hand, it is the life that touches us, and on the other hand, it is the word that tells us. Sometimes we are engaged in something which seems quite good according to doctrine, and our reason for doing it is also quite right, but within there is something which keeps touching us and will not let us go. Eventually, the Lord speaks to us; *rhema* comes, the mighty word of the Lord. It tells us that a certain matter must be dealt with and cleansed. On the one hand, this is the life, and on the other hand, it is the word of the Lord. By this we are cleansed. Sometimes the order is changed. At the beginning we do not feel anything while we are engaged in a certain matter; in fact, we feel that everything is fine. But when *rhema* comes, the word of the Lord speaks to us first, telling us that this particular matter is wrong, and then the life within us demands that we deal with it. This is our daily life. Either the life of the Lord does not allow us to do something, and the word comes; or first the word comes, and then the life follows, demanding that we deal with it. But it is always the cleansing of the water in the word to sanctify us.

Therefore, the whole matter of our growth and progress depends upon our attitude towards life and *rhema*. If we have any inner feeling in life, we should never let it go. We must pray, "Lord, please give the *rhema* that I might know how to deal with this situation." If the Lord first gives us *rhema*, speaking to us first, then we still need to ask Him to supply us with life to deal with the matter. If we pay attention to these matters and do not take them lightly, the Lord will cleanse us by the washing of the water in the word that we may be sanctified.

Before the Lord, the meaning of the church being cleansed by the washing of water is that the life of Christ deals with every part that is not out of Christ. The natural life and all that is not out of Christ must be purged away. Sanctification can only come after cleansing, and the basis of cleansing is the Lord's word, the *rhema*. If we do not know the Lord's word, there is no way for us to be cleansed and sanctified. Since the day we became Christians, from where has our knowledge come? Has it come from an outward source or from an inward one? Do we understand the will of God from within, or is His will still something outside of us? Many difficulties have their root in this very matter—the lack of God's word. The reason the Body of Christ cannot be built is because we merely have something outward, not something inward. The whole basis of the Christian faith depends upon the Lord's speaking. The growth of the church also depends upon the word which the Lord speaks. Therefore, the central point of our prayers should be our longing for the Lord's speaking. Oh, may the Lord speak to us! The Lord's word being spoken to us will enable us to attain the eternal purpose of God. The church today is not like Eve in Genesis 2, because the church has fallen. So the Lord must cleanse us by the washing of the water in the word.

The church according to God's will and the church in experience are two entirely different things. The church in God's plan is completely without sin; it has never known sin, nor had any history of sin. It is transcendent far above sin, without even a trace of sin. It is altogether spiritual and wholly out of Christ. However, the church in history has failed and is fallen. Today the Lord is working among fallen men to bring them back to the church of His original will. The Lord desires to work among people who are fallen, corrupted, and desolate, full of sin and filthiness, so that He may obtain a church from among them. He intends to restore and recover them to what He purposed in eternity past, so that He might have that which fulfills His desire in eternity future. In His magnificent work, the Lord is using the words He speaks as the instrument to bring the church back to God's original purpose. Oh, may we not lightly esteem the words of the Lord.

We must remember that knowledge is one thing and spiritual stature is quite another. All doctrine, teaching, theology, and knowledge are of little use if they just flow from one person to another. True growth depends upon our receiving the word directly from God. God is using His *rhema* to do His work, and He desires to speak to us. Therefore, if our purpose in reading the Scriptures is solely for knowledge, it is indeed pitiful. If this is so, we are finished. The real value of the Scriptures is that God can speak to man through them. If we desire to be useful in the Lord's hands, we must be spoken to by the Lord. Whether or not our building is spiritual depends upon whether the Lord has spoken to us. Knowledge and doctrine are of no spiritual use. Only the Lord's speaking in us is of spiritual value.

How can we ever be satisfied with knowledge and doctrines while the church is in a fallen state, when she has failed God and is blind to His will? May God have mercy upon us and be gracious to us! Oh, may we have such a prayer: "Lord, we pray that You would speak to us." All the words that are from without, all the words that are passed on to us by others, though they have been spoken a thousand or ten thousand times, are of no use. Only *rhema* is of any value. If we do something just because others tell us to do it, we are keeping the law; we are not in the New Testament. A person with a clear mind can divide the book of Romans into sections, such as "Salvation," "Justification," etc. But within him there is a great deficiency— God has not spoken to him. A man may have knowledge and yet be without God's word. Many people think that knowledge of the Scriptures and understanding of the doctrines are spirituality. There is no such thing! Bible knowledge can never be a substitute for spirituality. Only God's speaking to us, personally and directly, is of any real value. When God speaks to us through His word, we are enlightened; through His word we are sanctified; and through His word we are made to grow. We need to know what is dead and what is living, what is mere knowledge and what is spiritual. Whatever is not living has no spiritual value. If we have *rhema,* the living word of God, we can be cleansed and sanctified.

"THE CHURCH ... GLORIOUS"

What is Christ's purpose in His cleansing and sanctifying work? It is that one day "He might present the church to Himself glorious" (Eph. 5:27). Christ is waiting for the church to be prepared and presented to Himself. "The church...glorious" in the original language means that the church is brought into glory. In other words, the church will put on glory or be clothed in glory. Ephesians 4 says that the church will arrive at the oneness of the faith and the measure of the stature of the fullness of Christ (v. 13). Then chapter five says that the church will be clothed with glory to be presented to Christ. God intends to bring the entire church to this state. This is indeed a great matter! When we look at the condition of the church today, we say, "How can it be?" We may even doubt God's intention, but the Lord is working. One day the church will arrive at the oneness of the faith; she will arrive at the measure of the stature of the fullness of Christ; she will be clothed with glory and presented to Christ. This is what the Lord desires and will obtain. This is also what we desire and will obtain.

This glorious church will not have spot or wrinkle or any such things, but she will be holy and without blemish (5:27). The Lord will cleanse us to such a degree that it will seem as if the church has never had any spot or defilement. It will seem as if the church has never committed sin; nor will any trace of sin be found in her.

Not only is it without spot, but it is also without any wrinkle. We all know that children and young people have no wrinkles. Whenever wrinkles appear on a person, it means that he is getting old. The Lord wants to bring the church to the stage where there is nothing old, where there is nothing of the past. He wants everything in the church to be new. When the church stands before the Lord, it will seem as if she has never sinned, as if she has never had any history of sin. She will be without spot or wrinkle. In the future she will be the church according to God's purpose at creation.

The church will not only be without spot or wrinkle, but she will not have "any such things." In the translation from the Greek, it can be read, "This or that kind of defect." She will not only be without spot and wrinkle, but she will not have any defect whatsoever; all the defects will have been excluded. The day is coming when God's work upon the church will be brought to such a stage that she will be completely glorious.

Moreover, she will be "holy and without blemish." According to the meaning in Greek, this can be read, "That it should be holy and blameless." God will bring the church to the place where nothing can be said against her in any respect. The world will have nothing to say; Satan will have nothing to say; everyone and everything will have nothing to say; even God Himself will have nothing to say. In that day, when the church is so glorious, she will become the Bride of Christ.

We must see these two matters very clearly. First, today we are Christ's own Body. As His Body, Christ is purging and preparing us so that we may become the church which God intended from eternity. Second, when the time arrives, Christ will come, and we will be brought into His presence to be presented to Him as a glorious church, His bride. Therefore, first we have the history of the Body of Christ on earth, and then in glory the history of the bride. Now we are in the process of being cleansed. Now is the time that we need the *rhema*. Christians who have never received direct revelation are delaying God. If we have never heard the Lord speaking to us, we are hindering the Lord from pouring forth His grace. May God be merciful to us that we may not be those who hinder Him. Rather, may we be those who hearken to Him and go forward so that the church may be brought to the stage of being the Bride of Christ.

THE WORK AND RESPONSIBILITY
OF THE CHURCH BEFORE GOD

The book of Ephesians reveals the church which God has purposed in eternity. Chapter five tells how the church will be a glorious church, without spot or wrinkle or any such

things, holy and without blemish. Then chapter six speaks of
the practical work of the church, the spiritual warfare.

When we read Ephesians 6:10-12, we realize that the
work and responsibility of the church is spiritual warfare.
The opponents in this warfare are not flesh and blood, but
spiritual beings whose dwelling is in the air. Let us read
verses 13 and 14. "Therefore take up the whole armor of God
that you may be able to withstand in the evil day, and having
done all, to stand. Stand therefore." Here we are told that
we should stand, not that we should attack. The spiritual
warfare is defensive, not offensive, because the Lord Jesus
has already fought the battle and won the victory. The work
of the church on the earth is simply to maintain the Lord's
victory. The Lord has already won the battle, and the church
is here to maintain His victory. The church's work is not to
overcome the devil, but to resist him who has already been
overcome by the Lord. Her work is not to bind the strong
man—the strong man has already been bound. Her work is
not to let him be loosed. There is no need to attack; simply
guarding is sufficient. The starting point of spiritual warfare
is standing upon the victory of Christ; it is seeing that Christ
has already overcome. It is not dealing with Satan, but trusting in the Lord. It is not hoping that we will win the victory,
because the victory has already been won. The devil can do
nothing.

The church's work and responsibility is spiritual warfare.
It is a matter of the conflict between God's authority and
Satan's power. We come now to see the relationship between
the church and the kingdom of God.

Some people think that the kingdom of God simply
concerns the matter of rewards. This is too low of an estimate
of the kingdom of God. The Lord Jesus once explained what
the kingdom of God is. He said, "But if I, by the Spirit of God,
cast out the demons, then the kingdom of God has come upon
you" (Matt. 12:28). What is the kingdom of God? It is the
overthrowing of the power of Satan by the power of God.
When the devil is unable to stand in a certain place, the
kingdom has come to that place. Wherever the devil has been

cast out, wherever the work of the enemy has been displaced by God's power, His kingdom is there.

Revelation 12:9-10 says, "And the great dragon was cast down, the ancient serpent, he who is called the Devil and Satan, he who deceives the whole inhabited earth; he was cast to the earth, and his angels were cast down with him. And I heard a loud voice in heaven saying, Now has come the salvation and the power and the kingdom of our God and the authority of His Christ, for the accuser of our brothers has been cast down, who accuses them before our God day and night." We must pay attention to this word "for" in verse 10. The kingdom of God could come, "for" Satan had been cast down. Satan lost his place and could no longer stand there. At that time there was a loud voice in heaven saying, "Now has come the salvation and the power and the kingdom of our God and the authority of His Christ." Whenever Satan leaves a place, it is because the kingdom of God is there. Wherever the kingdom of God is, Satan cannot be there. This shows us clearly that in the Scriptures, the first, essential meaning of the kingdom of God is in regard to dealing with Satan.

When the Pharisees asked when the kingdom of God would come, the Lord Jesus answered, "The kingdom of God does not come with observation; nor will they say, Behold, here it is! or, There! For behold, the kingdom of God is in the midst of you" (Luke 17:20-21). What did the Lord mean when He said that "the kingdom of God is in the midst of you"? He meant, "I am standing here." Of course, we all know that the kingdom of God could not be within the Pharisees. On that day the kingdom of God was in their midst because the Lord Jesus stood in their midst. When He was there, Satan could not be there. The Lord Jesus said, "The ruler of the world is coming, and in Me he has nothing" (John 14:30). Wherever the Lord Jesus is, Satan must depart. In Luke 4 there was a man possessed by a demon. How did the demon react when he saw the Lord? Before the Lord said anything to cast him out, the demon cried out, "Ah! What do we have to do with You, Jesus, Nazarene? Have You come to destroy us?" (v. 34). Where the Lord is, the demons cannot be there. The very presence of the Lord Jesus represents the kingdom of God, and He is the kingdom of God. Where He is, the kingdom of God is also.

What does this have to do with us? Revelation 1:5-6 says, "To Him who loves us and has released us from our sins by His blood and made us a kingdom, priests to His God and Father, to Him be the glory and the might forever and ever. Amen." Notice the word "kingdom" in verse 6. This shows us that not only where the Lord Jesus is, but also where the church is, the kingdom of God is. Not only does the Lord Jesus Himself represent the kingdom of God, the church also represents the kingdom of God. The important point here is not a matter of future reward or position in the kingdom, whether large or small, high or low. The concern is not with these things. The vital matter is that God wants the church to represent His kingdom.

The work of the church on earth is to bring in the kingdom of God. All the work of the church is governed by the principle of the kingdom of God. The saving of souls is under this principle, and so is the casting out of demons and all other works as well. Everything should be under the principle of God's kingdom. Why should we win souls? For the sake of the kingdom of God—not just because man needs salvation. We must stand on the position of the kingdom of God whenever we work, and we must apply the kingdom of God to deal with the power of Satan.

The Lord wants us to pray, "Our Father who is in the heavens, Your name be sanctified; Your kingdom come; Your will be done, as in heaven, so also on earth" (Matt. 6:9-10). If the coming of the kingdom of God was automatic, the Lord would never have taught us to pray in this way. But since the Lord asked us to pray in this way, He simply showed us that this is the work of the church. Yes, the church should preach the gospel, but much more, the church should pray to bring in the kingdom of God. Some people think that whether or not we pray, the kingdom of God will come automatically. But if we know God, we will never say this. The principle of God's work is to wait for His people to move. Then He will move.

God told Abraham that the people of Israel would come out from the nation which afflicted them. However, this was not accomplished until four hundred thirty years later. When the Israelites cried unto God, He heard their cry and came to deliver them. Never presume that whether or not we cry things will happen in their own way. God needs man to cooperate with Him in His work. When God's people move, He will also move. When God's people saw that they should leave Egypt (though not all the Israelites realized this, yet some did), they cried to God, and He moved to deliver them.

Even the birth of the Lord Jesus was the result of the cooperation of some of God's people with Him. In Jerusalem there were some who were continually looking for the consolation of Israel. This is why the Lord was born. Although the purpose of God is to bring in His kingdom, His part alone is not sufficient. He needs the church to work with Him. Through prayer, the church must release the power of the kingdom of God upon the earth. When the Lord comes, the kingdom of the world will become the kingdom of our Lord and of His Christ (Rev. 11:15).

Since the work of the church is to stand for God and not give any ground to Satan, what manner of living should we have to accomplish this task? All our sins and unrighteousness must be dealt with, our consecration to God must be thorough, our soul-life must be put to death, and our natural man must be abandoned. The ability of the flesh is absolutely useless in spiritual warfare. "I" cannot resist Satan. "I" must go! Whenever "I" goes out, the Lord Jesus will come in. Whenever "I" enters, there is failure. Whenever the Lord comes in, there is victory. Satan recognizes only one person—the Lord Jesus. We cannot resist Satan. The fiery darts of Satan can penetrate our flesh, but, praise God, we can put on Christ who has won the victory.

We believe that Christ is going to come again. But do not think that the Lord Jesus will automatically come if we sit and passively wait. No, there is a work which the church must do. As the Body of Christ, we must learn to work together with God. We should never think that it is enough just to be saved. It is not. We must be concerned with God's need. There are two consequences of man's fall: one is the problem of man's moral responsibility, and the other is Satan's usurping of authority over the earth. On the one hand, man suffered loss, but on the other hand, God also suffered loss. Redemption solves the problem of man's moral responsibility and man's loss, but the loss which God suffered has not been solved. God's loss cannot be restored through redemption; it can only be restored by the kingdom. Man's moral responsibility has been dealt with by the cross, but the problem of Satan's authority must be dealt with by the kingdom. The direct purpose of redemption is for man, while the direct purpose of the kingdom is to deal with Satan. Redemption gained what man lost; the kingdom will destroy what Satan gained.

Man was originally given the responsibility to overthrow the authority of Satan, but instead man fell, leaving the authority to Satan. Man himself even became subject to him. Satan became the strong man, and man became his goods (Matt. 12:29). This situation demands the kingdom to deal with it. If there is no kingdom, then due to man's fall the work of Satan cannot be overthrown.

The new heaven and the new earth did not appear immediately after redemption was accomplished because the problem of Satan had not yet been dealt with. Before the new heaven and new earth come, there must first be the kingdom. Revelation 11:15 says, "The kingdom of the world has become the kingdom of our Lord and of His Christ, and He will reign forever and ever." Once the kingdom comes, eternity is ushered in. The kingdom connects with eternity. We may say that the kingdom is the introduction to the new heaven and the new earth. Revelation 21 and 22 show us that the new heaven and new earth appear after the kingdom. Isaiah 65 even describes the kingdom as the new heaven and new earth. This means that Isaiah viewed the kingdom as the introduction to the new heaven and the new earth. Thus, when the kingdom begins, the new heaven and the new earth begin also.

May God open our eyes so that we may not consider ourselves as the center. Why were we saved? Was it just so we should not go to hell? No. This is not the center. Why then did Christ want to save us? We can answer this question from two different viewpoints—from man's viewpoint and from God's viewpoint. When we view the same thing from two angles, it is seen in a different light. We should not just consider this matter from man's viewpoint. We must see it from God's viewpoint. In fact, the recovery of man's loss is for the recovery of God's loss. God's loss must be recovered through the kingdom. Today God has caused us to share the victory of the Lord Jesus. Wherever the victory of the Lord Jesus is displayed, there Satan must leave. We must simply stand steadfast, because the Lord Jesus has already won the victory. In His redemptive work, the Lord Jesus destroyed all the legal ground of the devil. All of Satan's legal rule has been terminated through redemption. Redemption was the sentence by which Satan was deprived of his legal position. Now the responsibility of executing this sentence is upon the church. When God sees that the church has sufficiently fulfilled this task, the kingdom will come, and the new heaven and the new earth will follow. The new heaven and new earth in the book of Isaiah will lead to the new heaven and new earth in Revelation.

Today we are standing midway between redemption and the kingdom. As we look backward, we see redemption; when we look forward, we see the kingdom. Our responsibility is twofold. On the one hand, we must lead the people of the world to be saved, and on the other hand, we must stand fast for the kingdom. Oh, may we have this vision so that we see the responsibility committed to the church by the Lord.

Let us review what the kingdom of God is. The kingdom of God is the realm where God exercises His authority. We must have such a kingdom among us. While we allow God to exercise His authority in the heavens, we must also allow Him to exercise His authority over us. God must have His authority, His power, and His glory among us. Not only must we seek to live before God according to Ephesians 5, but we must also pursue the responsibility revealed to us in Ephesians 6. Then we will not only be a church which is glorious, holy, and without blemish, but we will also be those who have cooperated with God to bring in His kingdom and caused Satan to suffer loss on this earth.

CHAPTER FOUR

"AND SHE BROUGHT FORTH ... A MAN-CHILD"

We have already seen the woman in Genesis 2 and how she speaks of the man whom God in His eternal will desires to obtain to glorify His name. Then in Ephesians 5 we saw another woman, who is the reality of the woman in Genesis 2. This woman shows how God is working to restore everything to His original purpose after man's fall. Now let us look in Revelation 12 at yet another woman. We must consider her in relation to the woman in Genesis 2.

Revelation is a book which reveals the things of the end time. There are a total of twenty-two chapters in this book, but by the end of chapter eleven we can say that everything is finished. Revelation 10:7 says, "But in the days of the voice of the seventh angel when he is about to trumpet, then the mystery of God is finished." In chapter eleven, when the seventh angel sounds his trumpet, everything concerning God's mystery and everything related to God is fully accomplished. Verse 15 says, "And the seventh angel trumpeted; and there were loud voices in heaven, saying, The kingdom of the world has become the kingdom of our Lord and of His Christ, and He will reign forever and ever." This means that when the seventh angel sounds his trumpet, eternity has already begun. The millennium, the new heaven and new earth, and everything regarding eternity are intimated in this verse. Why then are there still eleven additional chapters after the first eleven chapters? Our reply is that the following eleven chapters serve as a supplement to the first eleven chapters. Beginning with chapter twelve we are told *how* the kingdom of this world will become the kingdom of our Lord and of His Christ and *how* God will make His Son King forever and ever.

When the seventh angel sounds his trumpet, according to Revelation 11:19, something happens. "And the temple of God which is in heaven was opened, and the ark of His covenant was seen in His temple; and there were lightnings and voices and thunders and an earthquake and great hail." The book of Revelation contains many visions, but two central visions serve as the basis for all the others. The first is the vision of the throne (Rev. 4:2). All the visions from chapter four to chapter eleven, when the seventh angel sounds the trumpet, are based upon the throne. The second is the vision of the temple (Rev. 11:19). From chapter twelve to the end of the book, all the visions are based upon the temple of God.

In chapter four, John saw a vision of the throne of God with a rainbow around it. This signifies that from this chapter forward, everything is based upon the authority of the throne and the remembrance of the covenant which God made with every living creature on the earth. The rainbow is the sign of God's covenant which He made with all living things. At the present time we cannot see a complete rainbow. At most we see only half of it. But there is a rainbow that fully surrounds the throne. It is complete; there is no break in it. God is faithful; He will remember and keep His covenant. God will remember His covenant with every living creature on the earth. In everything that God desires to do toward man, He must abide by the covenant He has made.

At the end of chapter eleven, John saw another vision—a vision of the temple of God. Within the temple the ark of the covenant could be seen. God originally told the Israelites to build the ark according to the pattern which was given on the mount and to put the ark into the Holy of Holies in the tabernacle. Later, when Solomon built the temple, the ark was put into it. When Israel was taken captive to Babylon, the ark was lost. But even though the ark on earth was lost, the ark in heaven still remained. The ark on earth was made according to the ark in heaven. The shadow on earth disappeared, but the substance, the reality, in heaven still remains. At the end of Revelation 11, God once again shows us the ark.

What is the ark? The ark is the expression of God Himself. It signifies that God must be faithful to Himself. The throne is the place where God exercises authority, and the temple is the place where God dwells. The throne is something outward toward the world and mankind, but the temple is something for God Himself. The rainbow around the throne signifies that God will not do anything harmful to man, while the ark in the temple signifies that God will not do anything that comes short of Himself. What God has purposed, He must accomplish. What God desires to do, He is able to successfully perform. The ark was not only for man, but also for God Himself. God cannot deny Himself; He cannot contradict Himself. God purposed in eternity to have a glorified people, and He determined that the kingdom of this world would become the kingdom of our Lord and of His Christ. When we see the situation of the church today, we cannot help but ask, "How can God accomplish His purpose?" Yet we know that God will never stop halfway. He has the ark, and He Himself has made the covenant. The righteous God cannot be unrighteous with man. Furthermore, the righteous God can never be unrighteous to Himself. Man never does anything to contradict himself, for each man has his own character. Neither can God deny Himself in His work because of His own character. When God unveiled the ark to us, He meant that what He desires to do He must accomplish.

Here we must see one point. What is the basis upon which God and His Christ will reign forever and ever? What is the basis upon which God will cause the kingdom of this world to become the kingdom of our Lord and of His Christ? His character is the basis. God will accomplish all of these things because of His own character. Nothing can hinder Him. We must learn that whatever is of God can never be frustrated. The ark still remains, representing God Himself and His covenant. God will accomplish this matter by means of Himself. We thank God that from chapter twelve to the end of the book we are shown how God will accomplish all that He purposed in eternity through His own faithfulness.

THE WOMAN IN THE VISION

Revelation 12:1 says, "And a great sign was seen in heaven: a woman clothed with the sun, and the moon underneath her feet, and on her head a crown of twelve stars." Who is the woman described here? She is a woman over whom many Bible students have had much dispute. Some have said that she signifies Mary, the mother of the Lord Jesus. Others have said that she stands for the nation of Israel. However, according to the Scriptures this woman can neither be Mary, the mother of the Lord, nor the nation of Israel. Here are the reasons:

(1) Since this vision is revealed in heaven, this woman is entirely of heaven. Neither Mary nor the nation of Israel have this position.

(2) After this woman bore the man-child, she fled into the wilderness. If we liken this woman to the nation of Israel, the man-child she brought forth to Christ, and the man-child being caught up to the ascension of Christ, this does not correspond with the actual facts. Although the nation of Israel was scattered, her going into the wilderness was not the result of Christ's ascension. At the time Christ ascended, Israel had already been dispersed for some time and was no longer a nation. But here we see that the woman fled into the wilderness after the man-child was caught up unto God. Long before Christ ascended, the nation of Israel was gone. Therefore, it is impossible for this woman to be a reference to the nation of Israel. There is even less of a basis to refer to her as Mary.

(3) While this woman was in travail to bring forth the man-child, she encountered a dragon. This dragon had seven heads and ten horns. Chapter seventeen tells us that these seven heads are seven kings: five have fallen, one is still existing, and the other has not yet come. The ten horns are ten kings who have not yet received a kingdom, who will arise afterwards. We know that no such historical events occurred before Christ ascended. Therefore, this woman and the man-child must refer to things in the future. If we say that this woman refers either to the nation of Israel or to Mary and that the man-child refers to the Lord Jesus, we are contradicting history.

(4) After the man-child was caught up unto God, there was war in heaven, and Satan was cast down to the earth.

Then there was a proclamation in heaven: "Now has come the salvation and the power and the kingdom of our God and the authority of His Christ, for the accuser of our brothers has been cast down, who accuses them before our God day and night" (Rev. 12:10). We know that this has not yet been accomplished. Ephesians 6 tells us that the church on earth must still battle with the rulers, authorities, and spiritual forces of evil in the heavenlies. Satan is still there. Since this portion of Scripture has not yet occurred, it is impossible for it to be a reference to the time of Jesus.

(5) When the dragon was cast down to the earth, he persecuted the woman who brought forth the man-child. Many people use this as a confirmation that the woman is Mary. After Mary gave birth to the Lord Jesus she did flee to Egypt; however, she did not do this at the Lord's ascension. Verses 14 through 16 say, "And to the woman there were given the two wings of the great eagle that she might fly into the wilderness into her place, where she is nourished for a time and times and half a time from the face of the serpent. And the serpent cast water as a river out of his mouth after the woman that he might cause her to be carried away by its current. And the earth helped the woman, and the earth opened its mouth and swallowed the river which the dragon cast out of his mouth." Whether it is said that this woman is a reference to Mary or to the nation of Israel, we know from history that no such thing happened when Christ ascended to heaven. Therefore, this woman cannot be a reference to Mary or to the nation of Israel.

(6) There is one more proof. Verse 17 says, "And the dragon became angry with the woman and went away to make war with the rest of her seed, who keep the commandments of God and have the testimony of Jesus." After the man-child, who was born of the woman, was caught up to the throne, a remnant of her seed still remained upon the earth. This could not be Mary. Furthermore, this remnant keeps the commandments of God and has the testimony of Jesus. It is all right to say that the nation of Israel kept the commandments of God, but to say that the nation of Israel held the testimony of Jesus would mix the Old Testament with the New Testament.

In conclusion, it is impossible for this woman to be Mary or the nation of Israel.

Who then is this woman? The Old Testament shows that only one woman encountered the serpent—Eve in Genesis 3. In the New Testament there is also only one woman who encounters the serpent. Here we see the correspondence and correlation of the Scriptures, the beginning with the end. Furthermore, God particularly points out that the great dragon is the old serpent. This means that He is referring to the serpent who had been mentioned once before. God makes the point clear that it was that one and only old serpent. The emphasis is on the word "the"—*the* old serpent. Therefore, the woman mentioned here must also be that woman.

The sun, moon, and stars mentioned in Genesis 1 are mentioned in Revelation 12 in the same principle. As the serpent was in Genesis 3, so the serpent is here also. The seed of the woman mentioned in Genesis 3 is also mentioned here. Furthermore, the travail of birth is in Genesis 3, and it is also here. If we put these two portions of Scripture together, we can surely see that the woman in Revelation 12 is the woman whom God purposed in His eternal will. Everything that will happen to her at the end time is clearly stated here. The woman in Genesis 2 speaks of God's eternal purpose; the woman in Ephesians 5 speaks of the position and future of the church; and the woman in Revelation 12 reveals the things at the end time. In addition to these three women, there is another woman who shows forth the things in eternity.

When the woman appeared in the vision, the Scriptures pointed out firstly that she was "clothed with the sun, and the moon underneath her feet, and on her head a crown of twelve stars" (12:1). These facts are very meaningful in reference to the ages.

(1) The woman was clothed with the sun. The sun refers to the Lord Jesus. Her being clothed with the sun means that when the sun shines the brightest, it is shining upon her. In this present age, God is revealing Himself through her. This shows her relationship with Christ and the age of grace.

(2) The woman had the moon underneath her feet. This

phrase "underneath her feet" does not mean that she is treading upon it. According to the Greek, it means that the moon is subject at her feet. The light of the moon is a reflecting light; it has no light of its own. All the things in the age of the law merely reflected the things in the age of grace. The law was but a type. The temple and the ark were types. The incense, the showbread in the Holy Place, and the sacrifices offered by the priests were all types, as well as the blood of the sheep and oxen. The moon underneath the feet of the woman means that all things pertaining to the law are subordinate to her. This speaks of her relationship to the age of the law.

(3) The woman had a crown of twelve stars upon her head. The chief figures in the age of the patriarchs were from the time of Abraham to the twelve tribes. The crown of twelve stars upon her head speaks of her relationship to the age of the patriarchs.

In this way, we see that the woman is not only related to the age of grace, but also to the age of the law and the age of the patriarchs. However, she is more closely related to the age of grace. She includes all the saints in the age of grace, as well as all the saints from the ages of the law and the patriarchs.

THE BIRTH OF THE MAN-CHILD

Revelation 12:2 says, "And she was with child, and she cried out, travailing in birth and being in pain to bring forth." Being with child is figurative and not real. What does it mean to be with child? It means that a child is in the mother's womb, and the child and the mother are united in one body. When the mother eats, the child is nourished. When the mother is ill, the child is also affected. The condition of the mother is the condition of the child. The mother and the child are one.

However, this child is also different from the mother; he is another being. If you say that they are one, they are really one, for the child receives life from the mother. However, as far as his future is concerned, he is different. His future is entirely distinct from that of his mother. Immediately after he is delivered, he is caught up to the throne of God, while his mother flees into the wilderness.

In addition, while the woman is with child, all that can be seen is the mother; the child is hidden. Outwardly, it appears as if there is only the mother. The child assuredly exists, but he is hidden within the mother; he is included in the mother.

Verse 3 says, "And another sign was seen in heaven; and behold, there was a great red dragon, having seven heads and ten horns, and on his heads seven diadems." That serpent after several thousand years is completely different. Originally it was a serpent, but now it has been enlarged to become a dragon. What is the form of this dragon? It has seven heads, ten horns, and seven crowns upon its heads. It has the same appearance as the beast which rises up out of the sea. Revelation 13:1 says, "And I saw a beast coming up out of the sea, having ten horns and seven heads, and on his horns ten diadems." The beast which rises out of the sea also has seven heads and ten horns with crowns. This reveals Satan's goal—he wants to gain the crowns, which signify authority. The difference between the dragon and the beast is that the crowns of the dragon are upon its heads, while those of the beast are upon its horns. The heads signify the authority to decide, and the horns signify the authority to execute. The heads control and the horns execute. In other words, the horns are subject to the commands of the heads. Whenever the heads move, the horns follow. This means that all the behavior of the beast is under the control of the dragon.

Revelation 12:4 begins, "And his tail drags away the third part of the stars of heaven, and he cast them to the earth." Isaiah 9:15 shows that the tail denotes lying and deception. In Revelation 2 and 3, stars refer to angels. Since the stars of heaven are mentioned here, they are the angels. One third of the angels in heaven were deceived by the dragon, and they fell and were cast down with the dragon.

Verse 4 continues, "And the dragon stood before the woman who was about to bring forth, so that when she brings forth he might devour her child." Here is a woman whom God has purposed in His will and a man-child whom He desires to obtain. But the dragon is hindering what God is after in the woman. The dragon knows that this woman is about to bear a man-child; therefore, it stands before the woman and waits to devour her child as soon as she delivers.

Verse 5 says, "And she brought forth a son, a man-child." In order to see the relationship between the woman and the man-child, let us look at Galatians 4:26: "But the Jerusalem above is free, which is our mother." The last part of Galatians 4:27 says, "Because many are the children of her who is desolate rather than of her who has her husband." The Jerusalem that is above is the New Jerusalem, and the New Jerusalem is the woman, the goal which God desires to obtain in eternity. The woman in creation is Eve, the woman in the age of grace is the Body of Christ, the woman at the end of the age of grace is described in Revelation 12, and the woman in eternity future will be the New Jerusalem. When the Word says that the Jerusalem which is above has many children, it does not mean that the mother and the children are separate. It means that one has become many, and many are composed into one. The many children added together equal the mother. It is not as if the mother delivers five children, and then there are six individuals, but that the five children added together compose the mother. Each child is a portion of the mother— one portion of the mother is taken out for this child, another portion is taken out for another child, and so for each one. It seems as if they are all born of her, but in fact they are herself. The mother is not another being in addition to the children; she is the summation of all the children. When we look at the whole, we see the mother; when we look at them one by one, we see the children. When we look at the totality of the people in God's purpose, we see the woman; if we look at them separately, we see many sons. This is a special principle.

The same meaning is applied in Revelation 12 when it speaks about the woman delivering a son, a man-child. The man-child delivered by this woman is a wonder and a sign. The words "bring forth" do not mean that the child had his origin with her and was then separated from her, but merely that within her there is such a being. "She brought forth a son, a man-child" simply means that a group of people is included in this woman.

All of God's people have a part in His eternal purpose, but not all assume their rightful responsibility. Therefore, God chooses a group of people from among them. This group is a portion of the whole, a part of the many chosen by God. This is the man-child brought forth by the woman. As a whole it is the mother; as a minority it is the man-child. The man-child is the "brothers" in verse 10 and "they" in verse 11. This means that the man-child is not a single individual, but a composition of many persons. All of these persons added together become the man-child. In comparison with the mother, the man-child appears to be small. When the group is compared with the whole, their number is in the minority. But God's plan is fulfilled in them and His purpose rests upon them.

Verse 5 says, "She brought forth a son, a man-child, who is to shepherd all the nations with an iron rod." This speaks of the millennial kingdom. The overcomers are the instrument that enables God to achieve His purpose. Revelation mentions shepherding "the nations with an iron rod" three times. First, 2:26-27 says, "And he who overcomes and he who keeps My works until the end, to him I will give authority over the nations; and he will shepherd them with an iron rod." This passage quite obviously refers to the overcomers in the church. The last mention of this phrase is 19:15, which says, "And out of His mouth proceeds a sharp sword, that with it He might smite the nations; and He will shepherd them with an iron rod." This passage refers to the Lord Jesus. To whom then does the passage in chapter twelve refer? It must refer either to the overcomers in the church or to the Lord Jesus. Is it possible that it refers to the Lord Jesus? No. (However, it is not wholly impossible, for later we will see that the Lord Jesus is included here.) Why is it not possible? First, the man-child was caught up to the throne of God immediately after he was born. Therefore, this could not be a reference to the Lord Jesus. The Lord Jesus was not caught up immediately after He was born. He lived thirty-three and a half years on this earth, died, resurrected, and then ascended to the heavens. For this reason we believe that the man-child refers to the overcomers in the church. It is the portion of the people in the church who are the overcomers. The man-child refers to them, not to the Lord Jesus. (However, the man-child does include the Lord Jesus, since the Lord Jesus was the first overcomer and all overcomers are included in the Lord Jesus.) The man-child and the mother are different, and yet they are also one. The overcomers differ from the church, but they are included in the church.

THE RAPTURE OF THE MAN-CHILD

Revelation 12:5 continues, "And her child was caught up to God and to His throne." "Caught up" in this verse differs in meaning from "caught up" as it is used in 1 Thessalonians 4. There it says that some will be caught up in the clouds, while here it says that the man-child was caught up to the throne of God. The man-child was caught up to the throne because someone is already on the throne. The Head of the church is on the throne. God's purpose is not just to have one man upon the throne, but many men upon the throne. His original desire was to have a group of men on the throne to exercise His authority. God desires that Christ and the church together bring His purpose to fulfillment. However, the majority of the people in the church at that time will still not be able to attain the throne. Only a minority, called the overcomers, can go to the throne of God. They will be caught up to His throne because they will achieve God's purpose.

Two things occur immediately after the man-child is caught up: "And the woman fled into the wilderness, where she has a place there prepared by God so that they might nourish her there a thousand two hundred and sixty days. And there was war in heaven: Michael and his angels went to war with the dragon. And the dragon warred and his angels" (Rev. 12:6-7). Notice the word "and," which is used twice immediately after the man-child was caught up in verse 5. Verse 6 says, "*And* the woman fled into the wilderness...." Then verse 7 says, "*And* there was war in heaven...." The fleeing of the woman into the wilderness and the warfare in heaven are both due to the man-child being caught up.

Let us look into the matter of warfare in heaven. First there is Michael, whose name is quite meaningful. Michael means "Who is like God?" This is an excellent question. Satan's intention is to be like God, but Michael asks, "Who is like God?" Not only does Satan desire to be like God, but he also tempted man to be like God. However, Michael's question, "Who is like God?", shakes the power of Satan. It seems as if Michael is telling Satan, "You want to be like God, but you will never make it!" This is what Michael's name reveals to us.

Immediately after the man-child is caught up, there is war in heaven. In other words, the cause of the war in heaven is the rapture of the man-child. From this we see that the rapture of the man-child is not just a matter of some individuals being caught up, but more than that, it is to bring to an end the warfare which has been going on for ages and generations. The old serpent, the enemy of God, has been fighting against God for several thousand years. When this warfare takes place in heaven, Michael and his angels fight against the dragon, who is the old serpent. Formerly he was a serpent, but now he has changed in form to a dragon. He has steadily increased his power. However, once the man-child is caught up, not only is the dragon unable to be enlarged any further, but he is cast down from heaven. The rapture of the man-child is a transaction which causes Satan to have no more position in heaven.

What is the result of the fight between Michael and his angels and the dragon and his angels? Verses 8 and 9 say, "And they [the dragon and his angels] did not prevail, neither was their place found any longer in heaven. And the great dragon was cast down, the ancient serpent, he who is called the Devil and Satan, he who deceives the whole inhabited earth; he was cast to the earth, and his angels were cast down with him." The dragon's defeat is the outcome of this battle. There was no place for him in heaven; he and his angels were all cast down to the earth.

The death of the Lord Jesus has already dealt with the

position which Satan gained by man's fall. In other words, redemption has destroyed the legal position of Satan. The work of the church is to execute in the kingdom of God what the Lord Jesus accomplished in redemption and, consequently, to completely bring to an end the legal position of Satan gained by man's fall. Redemption is Christ's solution for the fall; the kingdom is the church's solution for the fall. The work of judgment was Christ's, while the task of executing this judgment rests upon the church. The overthrow of Satan is our work. God is trying to end this age. He needs overcomers. If there is no man-child, there will be no way to overthrow Satan's work. Satan has already been judged by redemption; now the punishment must be executed by the kingdom.

After the dragon and his angels were cast down from heaven, verse 10 says, "And I heard a loud voice in heaven saying, Now has come the salvation and the power and the kingdom of our God and the authority of His Christ." This is the kingdom. When Satan is cast down, when his angels are cast down with him, and when there is no place in heaven for them, this is the salvation, power, and kingdom of our God, and the authority of His Christ.

Let us read two verses in Revelation together. "And the seventh angel trumpeted; and there were loud voices in heaven, saying, The kingdom of the world has become the kingdom of our Lord and of His Christ, and He will reign forever and ever" (11:15). This is the subject. "And I heard a loud voice in heaven saying, Now has come the salvation and the power and the kingdom of our God and the authority of His Christ" (12:10). This is the successful fulfillment of the subject. The key to success is the rapture of the man-child. Because the man-child is caught up, there will be warfare in heaven and Satan will be cast down. The result of Satan being cast down is the coming of the kingdom of our Lord and His Christ. The rapture of the overcomers causes Satan to be cast down and introduces the kingdom. The work of the overcomers is to bring in God's kingdom. The Lord's work has been accomplished, and He is on the throne. Now the overcomers bring this into realization.

There is corresponding passage in Luke 10 which says, "And the seventy returned with joy, saying, Lord, even the demons are subject to us in Your name" (v. 17). The disciples had been casting out demons. Then the Lord said, "I was watching Satan fall like lightning out of heaven" (v. 18). This is a reference to Satan being cast down from heaven. But when does this event occur? It occurs in Revelation 12. What causes Satan to be cast down? According to Luke 10:18, which is based upon verse 17, Satan is cast down from heaven because the church casts out demons. Verse 17 also shows that casting out demons is not a once for all matter; rather, the church should continue to cast out demons on the earth so that Satan will be cast down from heaven. When the Lord Jesus died, all the power of Satan was destroyed. But what can actually cause Satan to lose his power in heaven? All of his power can be brought to an end by God's children on earth repeatedly dealing with him, instance after instance. When the demons have been subdued many times in the name of the Lord Jesus, Satan will be cast down.

Suppose that we have a balance that is used for weighing. On one side of the balance there is Satan. Since we do not know how much Satan weighs, we must keep adding weight on the other side of the scale. Each time we deal with Satan we add more weight to the other side. When the weight is increased to a certain point, Satan will be moved. In the beginning, as we continue to add weight to the other side, it is seemingly of no use. But each addition of weight is valuable. Finally, when the last amount of weight is added, the balance will start to move. We do not know who will add the last amount of weight, but all the weight, that which is added in the beginning and that which is added at the end, produces the effect. The work of the church is to resist the work of Satan so that together we can cast out the demons. This is why Satan will do anything in his power to hinder us from being overcomers.

Casting out demons does not necessarily mean that when we encounter a demon we should confront him. Casting out demons means that we cast out all the work and power of the demon. We lay hold of the authority of the Lord and stand fast in our position. One brother adds a little weight, and another brother adds a little more weight. Then one day Satan will be cast down from heaven. God does not work directly by His own hand to cause Satan to fall from heaven. It would be very easy for Him to do this work, but He does not. He has entrusted this work to the church. Oh, how pitifully the church has failed in this matter and been unable to do it! This is why there must be the overcomers standing in the position of the church to do God's work. When the overcomers stand in the church's position and do the work which the church should have done, the result will be: "Now has come the salvation and the power and the kingdom of our God and the authority of His Christ." The man-child in Revelation 12 consists of the overcomers who stand on behalf of the church. Therefore, as soon as the man-child is caught up, Satan is cast down from heaven and the kingdom comes.

THE PRINCIPLE OF THE MAN-CHILD

The Scripture says that this man-child will "shepherd all the nations with an iron rod." This is God's purpose. The work of the church is to cause Satan to lose his power and bring in God's kingdom. The church which God desires must have the characteristic of Abigail—that of cooperation with Christ. Since the church, however, has not attained to God's purpose, nor does she even know God's purpose, what can God do? He will choose a group of overcomers who will attain His purpose and fulfill His demand. This is the principle of the man-child.

There are many examples of this principle in the Bible. What was God's purpose in choosing the people of Israel in the Old Testament time? Exodus 19 tells us that He chose them to be a kingdom of priests. What does a kingdom of priests mean? It means that the whole nation was to serve God and be His priests. However, not all of the people of Israel became priests, because they worshipped the golden calf. Instead of serving God, they worshipped an idol. Therefore, Moses charged the people of Israel, saying, "Who is on the Lord's side? let him come unto me" (Exo. 32:26). Then all of the sons of Levi gathered themselves together unto Moses. Then Moses said to them, "Thus saith the Lord

God of Israel, Put every man his sword by his side, and go in and out from gate to gate throughout the camp, and slay every man his brother, and every man his companion, and every man his neighbor" (v. 27). The worshiping of idols is the greatest sin, so God required these men to slay their own brothers with the sword. "And the children of Levi did according to the word of Moses" (v. 28). They were willing to serve God above all their human affection, so God chose them to be the priests. From that time forward, only those of the tribe of Levi were priests among all the people of Israel. The whole body of the Israelites henceforth approached God through the Levites. Originally, all of the Israelites were chosen to serve God, but they failed Him; therefore, God chose from among the whole body of failures a group of people who would stand in their place. This group of people is the overcomers.

We must remember that the Levites did not serve God for themselves, nor were they overcomers by their own selection. Much less did they claim superiority over the others. If this had happened, they would have been finished. The Levites were chosen by God to be the priests as representing the whole body of the people of Israel. What the children of Israel should have offered unto God, the children of Levi offered for them. The service of the Levites before God was counted as the service of the whole nation of Israel. Only the children of Levi were priests, but the whole nation of Israel benefited from their priesthood. In the same manner, the work of the overcomers is for the whole church. The work belongs to the overcomers, but the church receives the blessing of the work. This is the glory of the overcomers. The business is theirs, but their accomplishments bring glory to the whole church; the work is theirs, but the whole church derives the blessing.

During the time of the Judges, the people of Israel were oppressed by the Midianites and were in great desperation. Out of one of their tribes, God raised up Gideon to lead a contingent of men and chase away the enemy. The whole nation was set free because of this group. The responsibility rested on the whole nation, but some were afraid and some were slothful; therefore, a group of them went forth to the battle and brought benefit to the whole nation.

The same principle is seen when the people of Israel returned from captivity. God originally promised that after the seventy years of captivity, the people of Israel would return and be restored to the land. However, not all returned; only a minority led by Ezra, Nehemiah, Zerubbabel, and Joshua came back to build the temple and the city of Jerusalem. But what they did counted for the whole nation of Israel. It was reckoned as the recovery and returning of the whole nation.

The principle of the overcomers is not that an individual who is especially spiritual will have a crown and glory waiting for him. This is not to say that individuals will not be rewarded with crowns and glory in that day. These they may obtain, but they are not for these; this is not their main purpose. The reason for the overcomers to be the overcomers is not to receive glory or crowns for themselves, but simply to take the position which the whole church should take and do the work for the church. Before God, the church should be in that condition which He desires; she should be responsible to Him, fulfilling the work committed to her and standing in her proper position. The church, however, has failed and is still failing today. She has not become what she was originally purposed to be; she has not done her work, taken up her responsibility, nor stood in her proper position. She has not gained the ground for God. There is only a group of people left to do that work for the church and to take up the church's responsibility. This group is the overcomers. What they do is counted as the work of the whole church. If there are those who will be the overcomers, God's purpose is attained and He is satisfied. This is the principle of the man-child.

The reason we are considering this matter of the man-child is because in God's eternal purpose He needs a group of overcomers. According to history, we have to admit that the church has failed. Therefore, God is calling the overcomers to stand for the church. The man-child spoken of in this passage of Revelation refers particularly to the overcomers at the end time. Once the man-child is brought forth, he will be caught up to the throne of God. Then things will immediately happen in heaven and Satan will be cast down. God's difficulty is removed by the rapture of the man-child; His problem is solved. It seems that once the man-child is born, God's purpose can no longer be hindered. This is what God is calling for today; this is what interests Him today. God needs a group of people to attain His original goal.

THE BASIS AND ATTITUDE OF THE OVERCOMERS

In Revelation 3:21 the Lord Jesus said, "He who overcomes, to him I will give to sit with Me on My throne." The reason the man-child can be upon the throne is because he has overcome. Now we will see how they overcome and what is their attitude.

Revelation 12:11 says, "And they overcame him because of the blood of the Lamb and because of the word of their testimony, and they loved not their soul-life even unto death."

"They overcame him." "Him" refers to Satan. They overcame Satan by rendering him unable to do any of his work upon them. They overcame him (1) because of the blood of the Lamb, (2) because of the word of their testimony, and (3) because they had an attitude of not loving their soul-life even unto death.

The Blood of the Lamb

First, "they overcame him because of the blood of the Lamb." Victory in spiritual warfare is based upon the blood of the Lamb. The blood is not only for forgiveness and salvation, it is also the basis by which we overcome Satan. Some people may think that the blood is not of much value to those who have grown in the Lord. They suppose that some may grow to the extent that they go beyond the need of the blood. We must emphatically say that there is no such thing! No person can grow to the extent that he surpasses the need for the blood. God's Word says, "They overcame him because of the blood of the Lamb."

The major activity of Satan against Christians is to accuse them. Is Satan a murderer? Yes. Is he a liar and a tempter?

Yes. Is he one who attacks us? Yes. But this is not all. His chief work is to accuse. Revelation 12:10 says, "The accuser of our brothers has been cast down, who accuses them before our God day and night." We see here that Satan accuses the brothers day and night. Not only is he the accuser before God, but he is also the accuser in our conscience, and his accusations can cause us to become weak and completely powerless. He likes to accuse people to such an extent that they consider themselves useless and thus lose all their ground for fighting with him. We are not saying that there is no need for us to deal with sin. We must have a keen sense toward sin, but we should not accept the accusations of Satan.

Once a child of God accepts Satan's accusations, he will feel that he is wrong all day long. When he rises early in the morning, he will feel that he is wrong. When he kneels down to pray, he will feel that he is wrong and does not even believe that God will answer his prayer. When he wants to speak a word in the meeting, he will feel that it is no use, because he is not right. When he wants to give an offering to the Lord, he wonders why he should offer anything, because God would surely not accept an offering from such a person as he. The main concern of Christians like this is not how glorious and victorious the Lord Jesus is, but how evil and worthless they are. From morning to evening they are consumed with the thought of their own worthlessness. Whether they are working, resting, walking, reading the Scriptures, or praying, a single moment does not pass without their consideration of how worthless they are. This is the accusation of Satan. If Satan can keep them in such a condition, he was won the victory. People in this state are powerless before Satan. If we accept these accusations, we can never be an overcomer. Often when we are engrossed with the thought of our own evil, it is easy for us to mistakenly consider this as Christian humility, not realizing that we are suffering the harmful effect of Satan's accusations. When we sin, we must confess and deal with it. But we must learn another lesson; we must learn to not look upon ourselves, but only gaze upon the Lord Jesus. Being conscious of our self every day from morning until evening is a sickly condition. It is the result of accepting the accusations of Satan.

In the consciences of some of the Lord's children there is little feeling toward sin. This kind of people are not of much spiritual use. However, there are many of God's children whose consciences are so weak that they have no real awareness of the work of the Lord Jesus. If we ask them if they have the sense of a particular sin, they cannot point to any. Yet they always have the feeling that they are wrong. They always feel that they are weak and worthless. Whenever they think of themselves, they lose all of their peace and joy. They have accepted the accusations of Satan. Whenever Satan gives us this kind of feeling, we are weakened and can no longer resist him.

We must not, therefore, lightly esteem the accusations of Satan. His chief work is to accuse us, and he does it day and night without ceasing. He accuses us in our conscience as well as before God until our conscience becomes so weak that it cannot be strengthened.

In the daily life and work of a Christian, the conscience is of great importance. The apostle Paul said in 1 Corinthians 8 that if one's conscience is defiled, he is destroyed. Being destroyed does not mean eternal perishing but that a person can no longer be built up. He has been so weakened that he has become worthless. First Timothy 1 says that a man who thrusts away his conscience is shipwrecked regarding the faith. A ship which is wrecked cannot sail. Therefore, whether or not a Christian can stand before God depends upon whether he has any offense in his conscience. Once he accepts the accusations of Satan, his conscience is offended, and once his conscience is offended, he cannot proceed in his service nor fight for God any more. We must realize, therefore, that Satan's main work is to accuse us, and this is the work we must overcome.

How can we overcome the accusations of Satan? The voice from heaven tells us, "They overcame him because of the blood of the Lamb." The blood is the basis of victory, and it is the instrument to overcome Satan. He may accuse us, but we can answer that the blood of Jesus Christ, God's Son,

cleanses us from every sin (1 John 1:7). "Every sin" means
any sin, whether it is great or small. The blood of God's Son
cleanses us from all of them. Satan may tell us that we are
wrong, but we have the blood of the Lord Jesus. The blood of
the Lord Jesus can cleanse us of our many sins. This is the
Word of God. The blood of Jesus, God's Son, cleanses us from
every sin.

We must not only reject the accusations which are without
cause, but we must also reject all the accusations which have
cause. When God's children have done something wrong, we
need only the blood of Jesus, His Son, not the accusations of
Satan. The precious blood is needed for sin, not accusation.
God's Word never speaks of the need for accusation after we
have sinned. The only problem is whether or not we have
confessed our sin. If we have confessed, then what more can
be said? If we have sinned and do not confess, then we
deserve to be accused. But where there is no sin, there is no
cause for accusation. If we have sinned and have confessed,
we should not be accused.

If you have sinned, you can bow and confess to God. Immediately the blood of the Lord Jesus will cleanse you. Do not
think that you will be a little more holy if you consider how
sinful you are, or that you will be more holy if you have more
feeling toward your sin. No. You only must ask yourself one
thing: How do I treat the blood of the Lord Jesus? We have
sinned, but His blood cleanses us from every sin. "Every sin"
means great sin or small sin, recollected sin or forgotten sin,
visible sin or invisible sin, sin which we think can be forgiven
and sin which we do not think can be forgiven—every kind is
included in "every." The blood of Jesus, God's Son, does not
wash us of one or two sins, or even many sins, but it cleanses
us from *every* sin.

We admit that we have sin. We do not say that we are
without sin. But regardless of this, we do not accept the
accusations of Satan. Before God we are clean because we
have the precious blood. We should not believe in the accusations more than we believe in the precious blood. When we
commit sin, we do not glorify God, but when we do not
trust the precious blood, we dishonor Him even more. It is a

shameful thing to sin, but not to believe in the precious blood is even more shameful. We must learn to trust in the blood of the Lamb.

Romans 5:9 says, "...having now been justified in His blood." When many people come into the Lord's presence, they have no peace in their heart. They also have a feeling of worthlessness and of being wrong within. This is because they have a false hope. They expect that they will have something positive in themselves to offer to God. When they discover that they do not have anything positive to offer in themselves, the accusations come. An accusation is like this: "A person like you will never have anything good to offer to God." But we must remember that we originally possessed no positive goodness before God. There was nothing good in ourselves that we could offer to God. We could only present one thing to Him—the blood. We could only be justified by the blood. We do not have any positive righteousness in ourselves. We become righteous only because of the righteousness which we receive through redemption. Every time we come to the throne of grace, we can look to Him for grace. It is a throne of grace, not a throne of righteousness. Every time we come before God, our only qualification is that we have been redeemed, not that we have advanced in our Christian life. No Christian can ever reach the stage where he can say, "I have been doing pretty well recently; now I have the boldness to pray." No. Every time we come before God, our only ground, our only position, is based upon the blood. We must realize that no amount of spiritual growth can substitute for the effectiveness of the blood. Not one spiritual experience can ever replace the work of the blood. Even if someone should become as spiritual as the apostle Paul, the apostle John, or the apostle Peter, he would still need the blood to stand before God.

Sometimes when we have sinned, Satan comes to accuse us, and sometimes when we have not sinned, Satan still comes to accuse us. Sometimes it is not a problem of whether or not we have sinned, but a problem of not having a positive righteousness to offer to God; so Satan accuses us. However, we must be clear: We can come into God's presence only because of the blood, not because of anything else. Since we have been cleansed by the blood and justified by the blood, we are under no obligation whatsoever to accept the accusations of Satan.

The precious blood is the basis for spiritual warfare. If we do not know the value of the blood, we cannot fight. Once our conscience is weakened, we are finished. Therefore, if we do not maintain a blameless and clean conscience, we will have no way to deal with Satan. Satan can use thousands of reasons in his accusations against us. If we accept them, we will fall. But when Satan speaks to us, we can reply to all his reasons with the one answer of the blood. There is not a single reason which cannot be answered by the blood. Spiritual warfare requires a conscience without offense, and the blood alone can give us such a conscience.

Hebrews 10:2 says, "Because those worshipping, having once been purified, would have no longer had the consciousness of sins...." When a Christian's conscience no longer has the sense of sin, it is because of the blood. Once we stand on the ground of the blood, once we believe in the blood, Satan can no longer work upon us. We often like to reason that we can no longer fight because we have sinned. But the Lord knows that we are sinful, so He has prepared the blood. The Lord has a way for sinful man, because the Lord has the blood. But He has no way for one who willingly receives Satan's accusations. Anyone who accepts the accusations of Satan denies the power of the blood. No one who believes in the precious blood can receive Satan's accusations at the same time. Either one or the other must go. If we accept the accusations, the blood has to go; if we accept the blood, the accusations have to go.

The Lord Jesus is the High Priest and Mediator for us (see Heb. 2:17-18; 4:14-16; 7:20-28; 8:6; 9:15; 1 John 2:1). He is always serving in this position—the High Priest and the Mediator. The purpose of His serving is to keep us from Satan's accusations. It takes only a moment of time for man to receive Him as Savior, but it is a lifelong matter to face the accusations of Satan. The word *mediator* in Greek means "an appointed defender." The Lord is our Mediator, our

Defender. The Lord speaks for us. But do we stand on the side
of the Mediator or on the side of the accuser? It would be
ridiculous if we believed the words of the accuser while our
Mediator is in the very act of defending us. If an attorney
continually proved that a defendant was not guilty and defendant persisted in believing the accuser, would that not be
quite absurd? Oh, may we see that the Lord Jesus is our
Mediator and that He is defending us. May we see that the
blood is the basis for us to deal with Satan. We should never
answer Satan's accusations with good conduct, we should
answer with the blood. If we realized the value of the blood,
there would be a great increase of peaceful and joyful Christians on the earth today.

"They overcame him because of the blood of the Lamb."
How precious are these words! The brothers overcame him
not because of their merit, their advancement, or their experience. They overcame him because of the blood of the Lamb.
Whenever accusations come from Satan, we need to deal with
them by the blood. Once we accept the blood, Satan's power
will be nullified. All that we are depends on the blood, and we
need the blood every day. Just as we depended upon the blood
and trusted in the blood on the day we were saved, we must
continue to depend upon the blood and trust in the blood from
that day forward. The blood is our only foundation. God
desires to deliver us from many senseless accusations. He
wants to break these chains. We must never feel that we are
being humble by receiving accusations day after day. We must
learn to overcome these accusations. If we do not overcome
accusations, we can never be the overcomers. The overcomers
must know the value of the blood. Although we do not know
the immense value of the blood, we can still say to the Lord,
"O Lord, apply the blood on my behalf according to Your
evaluation of it." We should deal with the power of Satan
according to God's valuation of the blood, not according to our
valuation of the blood.

The Word of Their Testimony

The second thing is that the brothers overcame him
"because of the word of their testimony." When our con-

science is without offense, then our mouth can give testimony. When there is an accusation in our conscience, we can utter nothing. It seems that the more we speak, the lower our voice becomes. The meaning of testimony here is to testify to others, not to one's self. When you have the blood before God, you will have boldness before God, and you will have a testimony before man. Not only will you testify that sinners can be forgiven and man can be accepted because of Christ, but you will further testify of God's kingdom. "Testimony" means to tell others what there is in Christ, and the word of testimony is something which must be spoken forth. The overcomers must frequently proclaim the victory of Christ. Satan fears the most when this fact is repeated again and again. It is a fact that the kingdom of heaven will come; it is a fact that the Lord is King; it is a fact that Christ is victorious and forever victorious; it is a fact that Satan is defeated; it is a fact that the strong man has been bound and legally condemned; it is a fact that Christ has destroyed all the work of Satan on the cross. When we declare all of these facts, we have the testimony. When we proclaim that Christ is this and Christ is that, this is the testimony.

It is the word of testimony that gives Satan the greatest fear. Satan does not fear when we try to reason with him, but he does fear when we proclaim the facts. Satan does not fear when we talk theology or when we expound the Scriptures, but he does fear when we declare the spiritual facts. "Jesus is Lord" is a spiritual fact. Many people speak about Jesus as the Lord and explain how Jesus is the Lord, but Satan is not afraid in the least. However, when someone declares in faith that Jesus is Lord, Satan fears. He does not fear our preaching or theology, but the word of our testimony.

It is a spiritual fact that the name of Jesus is above every other name. We must declare it in faith, not only to men, but also to Satan. We often speak for Satan to hear; we purposely speak for him to hear. We call this the word of testimony. Even when we are alone in our room we can proclaim aloud, "Jesus is Lord." We can say, "The Lord Jesus is stronger than the strong man," or, "The Son of God has already bound Satan," etc. This is the word of our testimony.

Christians must rely upon prayer in everything, but sometimes the word of our testimony is more effective than prayer. In Mark 11:23 the Lord Jesus said, "Whoever says to this mountain, Be taken up and cast into the sea, and does not doubt in his heart, but believes that what he says happens, he will have it." The Lord Jesus did not say that what a person prays will come to pass, but that what a person *says* will come to pass. The Chinese have a proverb which says, "A composition can come immediately from one's mouth." But Christians can say, "An accomplishment can come immediately from one's mouth." God created the heavens and the earth by one word of His mouth. The incident in Mark 11 shows us that we can speak to the mountain. Only if we speak in faith will something be accomplished. Many times the power of prayer is not as strong as the power of proclamation. Many times we must use the word of testimony to deal with Satan.

When we read the book of Acts, we can see many words of testimony. In chapter three Peter and John saw the lame man at the gate of the temple, and what Peter did was to say to him, "Silver and gold I do not possess, but what I have, this I give to you: In the name of Jesus Christ the Nazarene rise up and walk." This is what is called the word of testimony. It is not beseeching God to deal with the situation, but dealing with it directly in the name of the Lord. In Acts 16, when Paul cast out the demon, he also used the word of proclamation: "I charge you in the name of Jesus Christ to come out of her." Immediately the demon came out.

Let us further illustrate by relating a certain event. There were two sisters who were engaged in preaching the gospel. One day they came to a certain village and stayed for a while. A woman who was possessed of a demon was there, and a member of her family invited the two sisters to go to her home to cast out the demon. After praying, they felt that they should go. When they arrived, they saw that the woman was properly dressed and that everything was in good order. They wondered if the woman was really demon-possessed. Then they preached to her, and she seemed to be quite clear. (Actually demons cannot be clear, but they pretend to be.) The two sisters felt very strange about the situation. They asked the woman, "Do you believe in the Lord Jesus?" She answered, "I have believed for many years." Upon this reply, the two sisters were really confused; they did not know what to make of the situation. Then they asked her, "Do you know who Jesus is?" She said, "If you want to know who Jesus is, come and see." Then she led them from the front room to a room at the rear of the house. Pointing to an idol, she said, "This is Jesus. I have believed in him for many years." Then one of the sisters felt that she must give a testimony. Please note that what she said is the kind of testimony that we are talking about here.

The sister grasped the woman's hand and said (not to the woman, but to the demon), "Do you remember that more than nineteen hundred years ago the Son of God came from heaven to become a man for thirty-three and a half years? He cast out demons like you many times. Do you remember that you desired to attack and harm Him? You and all of yours rose up to kill Him and nail Him to the cross. You were very happy at that time. You did not know that He would rise from the dead after three days and break all your power. You are but a wicked spirit under the hand of Satan. Do you remember that when the Son of God came out from Hades, God announced from heaven to all living creatures and to all spirits, 'The name of Jesus henceforth is above every name. Whenever His name is mentioned, every tongue must confess and every knee must bow.' So I command you in the name of Jesus to come out from her!" When the sister made this proclamation, the demon cast the woman to the floor and left.

The sister's question, "Do you remember?" is of utmost significance. Her repeated urging of that question was her testimony. If we preach to Satan, he also can preach, and he can do quite a bit of it. If we reason with him, he has all kinds of reasonings. But if we speak the facts, especially the spiritual facts, Satan will be helpless.

We must know the facts in the Scriptures and believe them. We must be covered by the blood so that God may protect us from all the attacks of the enemy. Then we may speak to Satan. Satan fears when we speak the word of testimony to him. In our Christian experience, we sometimes feel so weak that we cannot even pray to God. At such a time we must remember the spiritual facts, the victorious facts. We must proclaim to Satan and his demons that the Lord Jesus is victorious and that Jesus is Lord. Such a proclamation is the testimony, and the testimony is the proclamation. What do we proclaim? We proclaim that Jesus is Lord, that the Lord is victorious, that Satan has been trodden under His feet. We further proclaim that the Lord has given us authority to tread upon serpents and scorpions and to overcome all the power of the enemy. This is the word of testimony. The word of testimony causes Satan to lose his ground. When we give the word of testimony, we give Satan a blow. The work of the Lord has not only given us the blood to protect us, but also the word of testimony by which we can defeat Satan.

Not Loving Our Own Soul-life

We have spoken of the basis of overcoming, but what is the experience of the overcomers themselves? They face trials and encounter many difficulties, yet Revelation 12:11 says, "They loved not their soul-life even unto death." This is the attitude of the overcomers in the warfare. In this verse the word "life" has two meanings. One denotes the physical life, while the other refers to the power of the soul. (The word "life" can be translated as "soul-life.") Let us consider the power of the soul or the natural ability.

The best way for Satan to deal with us is to cause us to act in our own strength. Satan wants us to move in ourselves. He wants us to exercise our own natural ability and fleshly energy in our work for God.

What is natural ability? Natural ability is the ability which we originally had and which has never been dealt with by the cross. It accompanies our character. The natural ability of one person may be his cleverness. In whatever he does, he draws upon his own cleverness. The natural ability of another may be his eloquence. He can speak well independent of any special power from the Holy Spirit. Man, however, cannot serve God with the natural ability that has never been dealt with by the cross. The failure of the church is due to man bringing in his natural ability. Oh, we all must be brought by God to the place where we are trembling and fearful lest we do anything without the Lord. We must become such persons—not merely *speaking* such things, but actually *being* such persons. Then we will become useful in the hand of God.

We are not encouraging anyone to pretend that he is holy. This is of no use, because it does not come from Christ. We are saying that God wants to break everything that is natural in a man. Only when we are cut off from all the elements that originate from our self will Christ be manifested. We must allow God to cancel the self through the cross. One day we must let God break the backbone of our natural life. We should not try to deal with this matter, piece by piece, item by item. For us to deal only with the outward things and leave the inward, natural life untouched is not only useless, but, on the contrary, it will make us proud. We will consider ourselves to be quite satisfactory, yet our inward condition will be even more difficult to deal with.

The day must come when our strength to do good and our ability to serve God are broken. Then we will confess before God and man that we can do nothing. Henceforth, Christ will be able to manifest His power upon us. We all must be brought by God to the place where we see that we can do nothing in the church with our natural strength. Many people think that as long as their motive is correct, it is good enough. But this is not the case. When you say you are working, the Lord will ask, "By what are you working?" If you say that you are zealous, the Lord will ask, "From where does your zeal come?" If you say that you have power, the Lord will ask, "What is the source of your power?" The question is not what you are doing, but with what you are doing it. The problem is not whether or not the matter is good, but what is the source of the goodness.

We must learn to experience the cross. The purpose of the cross is to deal with us, so that we will not dare to move by ourselves. It is useless merely to talk about the message of the cross or to listen to the message of the cross. God requires those who have gone through the cross and have been dealt with by the cross. It is not enough that our message is correct. We have to ask, "How about ourselves? What kind of persons are we?" The apostle Paul said, "For I did not determine to know anything among you except Jesus Christ, and this One crucified. And I was with you in weakness and in fear and in much trembling; and my speech and my proclamation were not in persuasive words of wisdom" (1 Cor. 2:2-4). The first part of these verses refers to Paul's message, and the last part refers to Paul's person. We often think that when a person like Paul gets up to speak he must feel rich and full of his own resources. But Paul's message was the cross, and he himself was in weakness, fear, and much trembling. Whenever we know the cross, we will be in weakness, fear, and much trembling. If we have been dealt with by the cross, we will not have any self-confidence, and we will not dare to boast. If we are proud, considering that we are quite capable, we know nothing of the cross.

The subjective work of the cross in us is to take away the things which do not originate with God. The cross leaves only the things which are of God. It cannot shake that which comes from God, but whatever is of man is powerless before it. Some brothers have said that in the past they had many ways to help people be saved, but after they began to experience the dealing of the cross, the cross has dealt with their various ways, and it seems as if they are not able to do anything. This proves that what they did previously came out from themselves, because whatever is of God cannot be slain by the cross. Anything that can be destroyed by the cross is certainly something of man. That which passes through the cross and rises up again is of God; anything which is not able to rise is of man. The Lord Jesus is of God, for after He passed through the cross, He was able to rise again. We should not love anything of the soulish life or of the life of the flesh, but let it all go into death. We must not allow anything of such a life to remain in us. The basis of our over-coming is the blood of the Lamb and the word of our testimony. Furthermore, our attitude is that we will not live by ourselves in any way; we will not value our own ability or have any self-confidence. We must live as men full of fear and trembling. We must realize what feeble creatures we are.

The other meaning of not loving our soul-life is that we do not love our physical life. We have to stand for God even at the cost of our life. In the book of Job, Satan told God: "Skin for skin! Indeed all that a man has he will give for the sake of his life" (2:4). Satan realizes that man values his life above everything else. But God said that the overcomers love not their lives. The attitude of the overcomer is that he does not care what Satan may do to him. Even though Satan would take his life away, he would never bow to Satan, but always remain faithful to God. The attitude of the overcomer is to be able to say to the Lord: "For Your sake there is not one thing that I would not forsake, even my life."

CHAPTER FIVE

THE HOLY CITY, NEW JERUSALEM

We have already seen that the woman in Genesis 2 is the same woman seen in Ephesians 5 and in Revelation 12. Now let us look at another woman, recorded in Revelation 21 and 22.

Although there is a long distance between them, the last two chapters of Revelation correspond with the first three chapters of Genesis. God created the heaven and the earth in Genesis, and the new heaven and the new earth are in the last two chapters of Revelation. In both Genesis and Revelation there is the tree of life. In Genesis there is a river flowing out from Eden, and in Revelation there is a river of living water flowing from the throne of God and of the Lamb. In Genesis there is gold, pearl (bdellium), and a kind of precious stone (onyx), and in Revelation there is gold, pearl, and all kinds of precious stones. In Genesis 2 Eve was Adam's wife. In Revelation 21 the Lamb also has a wife. The Lamb's wife is the New Jerusalem, and God's eternal purpose is fulfilled in this woman. In Genesis 3 man's fall was followed by death, sickness, suffering, and the curse. But, when the New Jerusalem descends from heaven in Revelation 21, there is no more death, sorrow, crying, or pain because the former things have all passed away. If we read the Scriptures carefully, we will see that Genesis 1 through 3 does indeed correspond with Revelation 21 and 22. They face each other at the two ends of the expanse of time.

Now we have seen four women: Eve in Genesis 2, the wife (the church) in Ephesians 5, the woman in the vision of Revelation 12, and the wife of the Lamb in Revelation 21. These four women are actually one woman, but her history can be divided into four stages. When she was conceived in the plan

of God, she was called Eve. When she is redeemed and manifesting Christ on earth, she is called the church. When she is
persecuted by the great dragon, she is the woman in the
vision. When she is completely glorified in eternity, she is the
wife of the Lamb. These four women reveal God's work from
eternity to eternity. The woman in Genesis 2 is the woman
purposed in God's heart in eternity past, and the woman in
Revelation 21 is the woman who fulfills God's purpose in eternity future. Of the two women in between, one is the church,
prepared for Christ by God, and the other is the woman who
will bring forth the man-child at the end time. In other words,
these four women show us the four stages of the history of one
woman: one stage is in eternity past, two stages are between
the eternities, and another stage is in eternity future. Even
though these four women appear to be different when we
speak of them separately, they are the same when we put
them together. The wife of the Lamb is the woman of Ephesians 5. Since the Lord Jesus is the Lamb, it is impossible for
the woman in Ephesians 5 to be anyone other than the wife of
the Lamb. The woman in Ephesians 5 is also likened to Eve,
and Eve is also likened to the wife of the Lamb in Revelation
21. When there are overcomers, whose work represents that
of the whole church, the woman in Revelation 12 will intro-
duce the woman in Revelation 21. As a result, God in eternity
future will indeed obtain a woman, a ruling woman who has
dealt thoroughly with Satan. God will truly obtain a wife for
the Lamb, and His purpose will be fulfilled. Let us see how
the woman of Revelation 12 becomes the woman of Revelation 21.

THE FALL OF BABYLON

Of the two women spoken of in Revelation 17:1-3 and
21:9-10, one is called the great harlot, and the other is called
the bride. Revelation 17:1 says, "And one of the seven angels
who had the seven bowls came and spoke with me, saying,
Come here; I will show you the judgment of the great harlot
who sits upon the many waters." Revelation 21:9 says, "And
one of the seven angels who had the seven bowls full of the
seven last plagues came and spoke with me, saying, Come

here; I will show you the bride, the wife of the Lamb." Revelation 17:3 says, "And he carried me away in spirit into a wilderness; and I saw a woman." Revelation 21:10 says, "And he carried me away in spirit onto a great and high mountain and showed me the holy city, Jerusalem, coming down out of heaven from God." When the Holy Spirit inspired man to write the Scriptures, He purposely used a parallel structure in pointing to these two women so that we would have a clear impression.

Let us first consider the things relating to the harlot. The harlot spoken of in Revelation 17 and 18 is Babylon, whose deeds are extremely displeasing to God. Why is her conduct such an offense to God? What does Babylon represent and what is the principle of Babylon? Why does God deal with Babylon and why is it necessary to wait until Babylon is judged before the wife of the Lamb appears? May God open our eyes so that we would really see Babylon according to the Scriptures.

The name *Babylon* originates from "Babel." We remember the story of the tower of Babel in the Bible. The principle of the tower of Babel involves the attempt to build up something from earth to reach unto heaven. When men built this tower, they used bricks. There is a basic difference between brick and stone. Stone is made by God, and bricks are made by man. Bricks are a human invention, a human product. The meaning of Babylon relates to man's own efforts to build a tower to reach unto heaven. Babylon represents man's ability. It represents a false Christianity, a Christianity which does not allow the Holy Spirit to have authority. It does not seek the Holy Spirit's guidance; it does all things by human effort. Everything consists of bricks baked by man; everything depends upon man's action. Those who are according to this principle do not see that they are limited; rather, they attempt to do the Lord's work by their own natural ability. They do not stand in a position where they are truly able to say, "Lord, if You do not give us grace, we cannot do anything." They think that man's ability can suffice for spiritual things. Their intention is to establish something upon the earth that will reach to heaven.

God, however, can never accept this. One man has some talent and thinks that he can preach after he has studied a little theology. What is this? Bricks! Another man who is very clever receives some help and possesses some knowledge and then becomes a Christian worker. Again, what is this? Bricks! A certain man is capable of doing things, so he is asked to come and manage the affairs of the church. What is this? Bricks! All of these things are man's endeavors to build something from earth to heaven by human ability, by bricks.

Again we must emphasize that there is no place for man in the church. Heavenly things can only come from heaven; the things of this earth can never go to heaven. Man's difficulty is that he does not see that he is under judgment, nor does he see that he is just dust and clay. Man may build high, but heaven is higher than man's highest height. No matter how high men may build their tower, they still cannot touch heaven. Heaven is always above man. Though man may climb and build and though he may not fall, he still will not be able to touch heaven. God destroyed man's plan to build the tower of Babel in order to show man that he is useless in spiritual matters. Man cannot do anything.

There is another incident in the Old Testament which out standingly manifests this principle. When the Israelites entered into the land of Canaan, the first person to commit sin was Achan. What was the sin which Achan committed? He said, "When I saw among the spoil a beautiful mantle of Shinar...I coveted them and took them" (Josh. 7:21). A Babylonian garment seduced Achan to commit sin. What does this beautiful garment imply? A beautiful garment is worn for the sake of appearance. When one puts on a beautiful garment, it means that he adorns himself to improve his appearance and to add a little luster to himself. Achan's coveting of the Babylonian garment meant that he was seeking to improve himself, to make himself look better. This was Achan's sin.

Who were the first ones to commit sin in the New Testament, after the church began? The Scriptures reveal that they were Ananias and Sapphira. What was the sin that they committed? They lied to the Holy Spirit. They did not love the

Lord very much, but they wanted to be looked upon as those who greatly loved the Lord. They were just pretending. They were not willing to offer everything cheerfully to God. Before man, however, they acted as if they had offered all. This is the Babylonian garment.

The principle of Babylon, therefore, is hypocrisy. There is no reality, yet people act as if there is in order to obtain glory from man. Here is a real danger to God's children—pretending to be spiritual. There is a great deal of spiritual behavior which is acted out in falsehood. It is put on as a veneer. Many long prayers are counterfeit; many prayerful tones are unreal. There is no reality, but it is made to appear as if there is. This is the principle of Babylon. Whenever we put on a garment which does not match our actual condition, we are in the principle of Babylon.

God's children do not know how much falsehood they have put on in order to receive glory from man. This is entirely opposite from the attitude of the bride. Everything done in falsehood is done in the principle of the harlot, not in the principle of the bride. It is a great matter for God's children to be delivered from pretending before man. The principle of Babylon is to pretend in order to receive glory from man. If we set our sight upon man's glory and man's position in the church, we are participating in the sin of the Babylonian garment and the sin committed by Ananias and Sapphira. False consecration is sin, and false spirituality is also sin. True worship is in spirit and truthfulness. May God make us true men.

Another condition of Babylon is seen in Revelation 18:7: "For she says in her heart, I sit a queen, and I am not a widow." She sits as a queen. She has lost all of her character of being a widow. She has no feeling about the Lord Jesus being killed and crucified on the cross. Rather, she says, "I sit a queen." She has lost her faithfulness; she has missed her proper goal. This is the principle of Babylon, and this is corrupted Christianity.

Chapter eighteen shows us many other things about Babylon, especially regarding the luxuries she enjoyed. Concerning our attitude toward the inventions of science, we can use many things when we have a need. Just as the apostle

Paul spoke of using the world (1 Cor. 7:31), our purpose with these things is simply to use them. However, luxurious enjoyment is another matter. There are some Christians who refuse all luxury and all things which contribute to the enjoyment of the flesh. We are not saying that we should not use certain things at all, but we are saying that anything in excess is luxury. Regardless of whether it is clothing, food, or housing, if it is excessive or beyond our need, it is luxury and in the principle of Babylon. God allows all that we need, but He does not permit things which are beyond our necessity. We should order our living according to the principle of need; then God will bless us. If we live according to our own lust, we are in the principle of Babylon, and God will not bless us.

We have seen that the principle of Babylon is mixing the things of man with the Word of God, and the things of the flesh with the things of the Spirit. It is pretending that something of man is something of God. It is receiving man's glory to satisfy man's lust. Therefore, Babylon is mixed and corrupted Christianity. What should our attitude be toward Babylon? Revelation 18:4 says, "And I heard another voice out of heaven, saying, Come out of her, My people, that you do not participate in her sins and that you do not receive her plagues." Second Corinthians 6:17-18 also says, "Therefore 'come out from their midst and be separated, says the Lord, and do not touch what is unclean; and I will welcome you'; 'and I will be a Father to you, and you will be sons and daughters to Me.'" According to God's Word, His children cannot be involved in any matter containing the character of Babylon. God said that we must come out from every situation where man's power is mixed with God's power, where man's ability is mixed with God's work, and where man's opinion is mixed with God's Word. We cannot partake of anything that has the character of Babylon. We have to come out of it. God's children must learn from the depths of their spirit to separate themselves from Babylon and to judge all her actions. If we do this, we will not be condemned together with Babylon.

Babylon had her beginning in the tower of Babel. Day by day Babylon is becoming larger and larger. But God will judge her in the end. Revelation 19:1-4 says, "After these things I heard as it were a loud voice of a great multitude in heaven, saying, Hallelujah! The salvation and the glory and the power are of our God. For true and righteous are His judgments; for He has judged the great harlot who corrupted the earth with her fornication, and He avenged the blood of His slaves at her hand. And a second time they said, Hallelujah! And her smoke goes up forever and ever. And the twenty-four elders and the four living creatures fell down and worshipped God, who sits upon the throne, saying, Amen, Hallelujah!" When God judges the harlot and shatters all her work, and when He casts out all that she is and the principle she represents, voices from heaven will say, "Hallelujah!" In the New Testament, there are very few hallelujahs, and they are all expressed in this chapter because Babylon, she who adulterated the Word of Christ, has been judged.

The passage in Revelation 18:2-8 tells us the reason for Babylon's fall and judgment. The sinful deeds of Babylon are announced and the consequences of her judgment are set forth. All who are of the same mind with God must say, Hallelujah, for God has judged Babylon. Though the actual judgment is in the future, the spiritual judgment must take place today. The actual judgment will be performed by God in the future, but the spiritual judgment must be made by us today. If God's children bring many unspiritual things into the church, how do we feel about it? Does the fact that we are all God's children and the fact that we should love one another mean that we should not say, Hallelujah, to God's judgment? We must realize that this is not a matter of love, but a matter of God's glory. The principle of Babylon is confusion and uncleanness; therefore, her name is the harlot. The few passages in Revelation which God uses to describe Babylon show us His exceeding hatred toward her. "Those who destroy the earth" in Revelation 11:18 are of this woman, of whom it is written in chapter nineteen that she "corrupted the earth" (v. 2).

God hates the principle of Babylon more than anything else. We must note in His presence how much of our being is still not absolute for Him. Anything which is halfway and not absolute is called Babylon. We need God to enlighten us so that in His light we may judge everything in us which is not absolute toward Him. Only when we judge ourselves in this way can we confess that we too hate the principle of Babylon. By His grace, may the Lord not allow us to seek any glory and honor outside of Christ. The Lord requires that we delight and seek to be one who is absolute, not one who is living in the principle of Babylon.

Revelation 19:5 says, "And a voice came out from the throne, saying, Praise our God, all His slaves and those who fear Him, the small and the great." A special feature of the book of Revelation is the proclamations from heaven. We read such things as a "voice out of heaven" and "a voice came out from the throne" (18:4; 19:5). These are declarations from heaven, signifying the time when God speaks, the place where God speaks, and what His emphasis is on. There are definite reasons for the proclamation in Revelation 19:5. On the one hand, it is because the great harlot is judged, and on the other hand, it is looking toward the marriage of the Lamb which is to come. Therefore, there is a proclamation from the throne to give praise to our God. God has been working from eternity and has expended much energy on His work so that He might obtain praise. Ephesians mentions that God has an inheritance in the saints. What is God's inheritance in the saints? There is only one thing that man can render to God—praise. Praise is God's inheritance in the saints. The voice from heaven proclaims that all of God's servants, all who belong to God, both small and great, must praise Him. God's purpose must be fulfilled, and it will be soon. God must obtain what He is after; we all must praise Him.

When the voice from the throne declared that praise be given to God, there was a host of echoes resounding throughout the universe. Revelation 19:6 says, "And I heard as it were the voice of a great multitude and like the sound of many waters and like the sound of mighty thunders, saying, Hallelujah! For the Lord our God the Almighty reigns." On one hand, there was a declaration from the throne, and on the other hand, there was a response of thousands upon thousands, and ten thousands upon ten thousands. As John was listening, he did not hear the voice of a single person; rather, he heard the voice of a great multitude as if it were the voice of many waters and the voice of mighty thunders. When you listen to the noise of a great waterfall or the waves of the ocean, you will realize how loud a voice of many waters can be. The voice of thunder is great enough; how much greater is the voice of mighty thunders! All of these mighty and thunderous voices were saying, Hallelujah! The declaration from heaven, the response from the whole universe, and every voice was saying, Hallelujah, because of a special event which was about to take place. The event is "the Lord our God the Almighty reigns."

As we read this proclamation, what are our hearts set upon? This passage does not say that *we* will reign and that we should therefore rejoice and be exceeding glad. Neither does it say that we will receive a crown and that we should therefore praise God. It says that the Lord our God the Almighty reigns. God's mind is that He should reign, that He should exercise authority. When God rules, it is Christ who rules. Let us turn back to Revelation 11:15: "The kingdom of the world has become the kingdom of our Lord and of His Christ, and He will reign forever and ever." "Our Lord" refers to God, and "His Christ" refers to Christ. But the pronoun "He" which follows is used rather strangely. Since the passage begins with "our Lord and...His Christ," it seems logical to continue with the phrase, "And *they* will reign forever and ever." This would be grammatically correct. But it is not written in this way. It is followed by the phrase, "And *He* will reign forever and ever." This enables us to understand that the Lord's reign is Christ's reign, and Christ's reign is God's reign. The kingdom of God is the kingdom of Christ. The reigning of God is the reigning of Christ. Because God reigns and Christ reigns, everyone rejoices with exceeding gladness and shouts, Hallelujah!

Revelation 19:7 continues, "Let us rejoice and exult, and let us give the glory to Him...." This is the time when God will be glorified. Following this, the verse says, "...for the marriage of the Lamb has come, and His wife has made herself ready." (*Wife* is the correct translation, though some

translators use *bride*.) Not only has God's authority com-
menced, but the kingdom has been ushered in. Furthermore,
the corporate man, the eternal Eve whom God desired, has
been obtained. The marriage of the Lamb has come, and His
wife has made herself ready. There are two reasons for
praise. First, God reigns. To this we say, Hallelujah! Second,
God has obtained what He determined to have in eternity
past. To this we also say, Hallelujah! We too should rejoice
and be exceeding glad, because one day God will surely obtain
what He desires. When the marriage of the Lamb has come,
the wife has made herself ready.

When we look at ourselves, it seems impossible that such
a day will ever come when Christ presents a glorious church
to Himself, not having spot or wrinkle or any such things.
But since this will happen, how can we refrain from saying,
Hallelujah! Regardless of how much weakness there has
been, both yesterday and today, God will obtain His determined will in that day. Never forget this—in that day the wife
will be ready. Therefore, we must give Him the glory, and we
must say, Hallelujah!

Let us read verse 7 again: "Let us rejoice and exult, and let
us give the glory to Him, for the marriage of the Lamb has
come, and His wife has made herself ready." We must take
note that this passage refers to the wife of the Lamb, not to
the bride of the Lamb. Now let us go on to 21:1-2: "And I saw a
new heaven and a new earth....And I saw the holy city, New
Jerusalem, coming down out of heaven from God, prepared as
a bride adorned for her husband." When do the events in
chapter nineteen, concerning the wife who has made herself
ready, occur? It is before the millennium. When do the events
in chapter twenty-one, concerning the bride who is ready,
occur? It is after the millennium. Since the New Jerusalem
must wait for the new heaven and new earth before it is the
bride of the Lamb, why does it say that the wife of the Lamb
is ready *before* the millennium? Please note that chapter
nineteen does not speak of the marriage of the Lamb, it
simply says that the marriage of the Lamb has come. At
that time, if we look back, we will see that the harlot has
fallen, and if we look forward, we will see the new heaven and

the new earth. Therefore, the declaration that the marriage of the Lamb has come is made. In reality, however, there are one thousand years in between. Only when these one thousand years have passed will the actual time for the marriage of the Lamb come. The woman is actually the wife of Christ in the new heaven and new earth, not during the time of the kingdom.

There is one more thing which we must notice. In chapter twelve there is the woman with the man-child and many other children. But in chapter nineteen there is only the wife. Where are the man-child and the many children? It seems as if they have disappeared. How can the woman, the man-child, and the rest of her children become the wife of the Lamb?

In order to be clear, we must look at the principle of the man-child. Remember that the man-child accomplishes everything as if representing the whole church. In chapter nineteen, the declaration that the wife has made herself ready is spoken while looking upon the overcomers. The whole body of the church must wait until the time of the new heaven and the new earth to be the bride. She will not be ready until then. But one thousand years prior to this, there is an announcement that the wife has made herself ready. Why is this spoken? What kind of readiness is there? This proclamation refers to the readiness of the overcomers and to no one but the overcomers. Because the overcomers are fully ready, a declaration can be made that the wife has made herself ready.

We must bear in mind that what the overcomers accomplish is not for themselves alone, but for the whole church. The Word of God says that when one member is glorified, all the members rejoice with it (1 Cor. 12:26). The overcomers war with Satan on behalf of the whole Body. Their victory brings benefit to the whole. Therefore, the readiness mentioned in chapter nineteen has to do with the matter of life. Because the overcomers have more maturity of life, they are ready. Because the overcomers are ready before God, He reckons their readiness as the readiness of the whole Body.

Do we sense the preciousness of this? We must remember this one thing—all of our seeking and all of our growth is not for us as individuals, but for the Body. What each member receives from God is for the whole Body. When your ears hear a word, you cannot say that *you* have not heard, because your ears are united to your body. When your mouth says something wrong, you cannot deny that *you* have spoken wrongly, because your mouth and body are united. In the same way, whatever the overcomers accomplish is the accomplishment of the whole Body. Since our Lord is the Head of the church, whatever He has accomplished on the cross belongs to the church. Likewise, as we receive benefit from the Head, we also receive benefit from the Body. As we partake of what the Lord has accomplished, we also partake of what the other members have accomplished. When God sees the readiness of the overcomers, He reckons it as the readiness of the whole church. Therefore, it can be said that the wife has made herself ready.

The readiness of the wife especially refers to the garments of the wife. Verse 19:8 says, "And it was given to her that she should be clothed in fine linen, bright and clean; for the fine linen is the righteousnesses of the saints." The Scriptures reveal that there are two kinds of garments for Christians. One is the Lord Jesus. The Lord Jesus is our clothing. The other is the fine linen garment, bright and clean, spoken of in verse 8. Whenever we come before God, the Lord Jesus is our garment. He is our righteousness, and we put Him on when we approach God. This garment is our common clothing; every saint is clothed before God and cannot be found naked. On the other hand, when we are presented to Christ, we must be arrayed with fine linen, bright and clean. This is the righteousnesses of the saints. "Righteousnesses" means a succession of righteous deeds, one after another. All of these righteous deeds together are our fine linen garment. When we were saved, we began to obtain a fine linen garment for our adornment—the righteousnesses of the saints.

We can also see these two sets of garments for the Christian in Psalm 45. Verse 13 says, "The King's daughter is all glorious within the royal abode; / Her garment is a woven work inwrought with gold." The material of her clothing is gold, beaten gold. Then verse 14 says, "She will be led to the King in embroidered clothing." The clothing mentioned in verse 13 differs from that in verse 14. In verse 13 the clothing is of gold, but in verse 14 the clothing is of embroidered work. The fine linen garments in Revelation 19 are embroidered, they are not of gold.

What then is gold? The Lord Jesus is gold. He is gold because He is entirely of God. The righteousness which the Lord Jesus gave us, the clothing which He put upon us when we were saved was something of gold. Besides this clothing, we have been embroidering another garment from the day we received our salvation. This relates to the righteous acts of the saints. In other words, the clothing of gold is given to us by God through the Lord Jesus, while the clothing of embroidered work is given to us by the Lord Jesus through the Holy Spirit. When we believed in the Lord, God gave us a gold garment through the Lord Jesus. This garment is the Lord Jesus Himself, and it has nothing whatsoever to do with our conduct. It was furnished by Him, ready-made. The embroidered garment, however, is related to our deeds. It is wrought one stitch at a time by the working of the Holy Spirit in us day by day.

What is the meaning of embroidery? Originally, there is a plain piece of material with nothing upon it. Later, something is sewed into it with thread, and by this sewing work, the original material and the thread become one. This means that when the Spirit of God works upon us, He constitutes Christ into us—this is the embroidery work. Then we will not only have a garment of gold, but also a garment embroidered by the Holy Spirit. By this work Christ will be constituted in us and expressed from us. This embroidered garment is the righteous acts of the saints. It is not done once for all, but repeatedly carried on day after day until God says that it is ready.

Perhaps some may ask what the righteous acts are that are specifically spoken of here. The Gospels record many righteous acts, such as Mary's act of expressing her love to the Lord by anointing Him with ointment. This righteousness may be one of the crosswise or lengthwise threads in her fine linen garment. There were others, such as Joanna, the wife of Chuza, and many other women, who because of their love for the Lord ministered to His material needs and those of His disciples. These also are righteous acts. Our heart is often touched by the love of the Lord, and we make an outward expression of it. This is our righteousness, our fine linen garment. This is the embroidering work which is being done today. Any expression which results from our love for the Lord and which is done through the Holy Spirit is a stitch among the thousands of other stitches in the embroidery work. The Bible tells us that whoever will give only a cup of cold water unto a little one will by no means lose his reward. This is a righteous act done out of love for the Lord. When we have some expression or act of love for the Lord, it is righteousness.

Revelation 7:9 says that the garment is a white robe. It has been washed and made white in the blood of the Lamb. We must remember that we can only be made white by being cleansed from our sins through the blood. Not only must we be cleansed from our sins, but we must also be cleansed from our good behavior. It too can only be made white by being washed in the blood. Not a single deed of any Christian is originally white. Even if we have some righteousness, it is mixed and not pure. We often have been kind to others, but inwardly we have been unwilling. We often have been patient with others, but when we have gone home we have murmured. Therefore, after having done some righteous deed, we still need the cleansing of the blood. We need the blood of the Lord Jesus to cleanse us from the sins we commit, and we also need the blood of the Lord Jesus to cleanse our righteous acts.

No Christian can ever make a garment which is pure white. Even if we could make one which was ninety-nine percent pure, there would still be one percent of mixture. Before God no man is entirely without blemish. Even good deeds done out of our love for the Lord need the cleansing of the blood. A very spiritual man once said that even the tears he shed for sin needed to be washed by the blood. Oh, even tears of repentance need to be cleansed by the blood! Therefore, Revelation 7:14 indicates that their robes were made white in the blood of the Lamb. We have nothing of which we can boast. From the outside to the inside, nothing is entirely pure. The more we know ourselves, the more we will realize how filthy we are. Our best deeds and our best intentions are mixed with filthiness. Without the cleansing of the blood, it is impossible to be white.

But the garments are not only white, they are bright or shining (19:8). The meaning of bright is shining. Whiteness has a tendency to become dull, pale, and ordinary. But this garment is not only white, but shining. Before Eve sinned, she might have been white, but by no means was she shining. Before the fall Eve was sinless, but she was only innocent, not holy. God does not merely require that we be white, but also that we be shining. Whiteness is a passive, quiescent aspect, but brightness is a positive, active aspect.

Therefore, we must not be afraid of hardship, neither must we long for a smooth pathway, because days of difficulty can make us shine. With some Christians we do not sense that they have sinned or that they are wrong in any way. On the contrary, we feel that they are quite good in almost every aspect. But we also do not sense any brightness. Their goodness is just ordinary goodness. They are white, but they do not shine. However, there are other Christians who are frequently tried and faced with suffering. Often they are so shaken that it seems as if they will surely fall—but they continue to stand. After a certain period of time these Christians attain a shining quality. They are shining in their character and in their virtue. They are not plain, but shining; they are not only white, they are bright.

God is working in us all the time. He is continually expending much effort upon us so that we may be white, and He is continually laboring upon us to make us shining. His desire is for us to be bright. Therefore, we must pay a great price. We must be willing for every kind of difficulty to come upon us. Otherwise, we can never be bright. Merely being white is not enough; God requires a positive brightness to be seen in us. The fear of hardship, the fear of trouble, and the longing for an easy way and a smooth path will cause us to lose our brightness. The more sufferings and difficulties we encounter, the more we can shine. People whose lives are spent in an easy and ordinary way may be white, but they will never be shining.

This garment is of fine linen. According to the Scriptures, wool has a different meaning than linen. Wool denotes the work of the Lord Jesus and fine linen denotes the work of the Holy Spirit. Isaiah 53:7 describes the Lord Jesus as a sheep that is dumb before its shearers. From this verse we can see that wool possesses the character of redemption. However, there is no character of redemption involved with fine linen. It is produced from a plant; it is not associated with blood. Fine linen is the product of the Holy Spirit's work within man. The fine linen garment tells us that God not only requires man to have God's righteousness, but also his own righteous deeds. God not only intends to obtain His righteousness in us, but He also intends to obtain many righteousnesses in us.

"And it was given to her that she should be clothed in fine linen, bright and clean" (Rev. 19:8). All the deeds, all the outward righteousnesses, are produced by grace. "It was given to her..." The deeds are not manufactured by the natural man, they are the product of the Holy Spirit's work in man. We must learn to look to the Lord and expectantly say, "Lord, give it to me. Lord, grant me the grace." How good this is—the garment is given by grace! If we say that the garment is made by us, this is true; it has indeed been wrought by us. But on the other hand, it is given by God, because we cannot produce a thing when we depend upon ourselves. The Lord accomplishes it in us through the Holy Spirit.

Many times we feel that a burden is indeed great. We want to escape, almost pleading with the Lord, "O Lord, release me!" But we have to change our prayer and say, "Lord, make me able to carry the burden. Lord, cause me to stand up beneath it. Make me white and grant me to be clothed in a shining garment."

Revelation 19:9 says, "And he [the angel] said to me, Write...." God spoke, and He asked John to write it down. What did he write? "Blessed are they who are called to the marriage dinner of the Lamb." The angel said, "These are the true words of God." Oh, there can be no other privilege, no other position higher than this—to be called to the marriage dinner of the Lamb. "These are the true words of God." God makes it especially clear that these are His true words. We must accept them, we must heed them, and we must remember them.

What is the difference between those who are called to the marriage dinner and the bride of the Lamb? The bride is a chosen group—the new man. But those who are called to the marriage dinner are a great many individuals—the overcomers. The marriage dinner of the Lamb refers to the age of the kingdom. Those who are called will be together with the Lord enjoying a unique and special fellowship, which no one has ever tasted before. The Lord said through the angel, "Blessed are they who are called to the marriage dinner of the Lamb.... These are the true words of God." May God cause us, for His sake, to be able to enjoy this special fellowship with Him. May He make us those who will humbly seek to satisfy His heart's desire. May He cause us to seek to be those who supply life for the sake of the church. And may He cause us and enable us to be the overcomers for the sake of the kingdom.

THE NEW HEAVEN AND THE NEW EARTH

Verse 21:1 says, "And I saw a new heaven and a new earth; for the first heaven and the first earth passed away, and the sea is no more." Here again, from a distance, we are standing opposite to Genesis. In Genesis 1, the heaven and the earth are the original heaven and earth, but in this verse we have a new heaven and a new earth. In Genesis there was the sea, but in this verse the sea is no more.

Verse 2 continues, "And I saw the holy city, New Jerusalem, coming down out of heaven from God, prepared as a bride adorned for her husband." In chapter nineteen there is a declaration that the marriage of the Lamb has come and His wife has made herself ready. But in this chapter, the New Jerusalem is prepared as a bride adorned for her husband. This is the actuality. There are many declarations in

Revelation, but the most important declaration is Revelation 11:15. According to the order of occurrence, the rapture of the man-child and the casting down of the dragon from heaven take place after this declaration. Then how can the words, "The kingdom of the world has become the kingdom of our Lord and of His Christ," be spoken at this time? It is possible because this declaration was made at the beginning of things, not at the point of their accomplishment. This means that a turning point has come. When there is a definite turn towards God's eternal purpose, God can make such a declaration in heaven. In chapter nineteen God makes another declaration, saying that the marriage of the Lamb has come and that His wife has made herself ready. This declaration is also made at the starting point of events which are about to occur. Because before Him the overcomers represent the bride and because this group of people is ready in His sight, God is able to declare that the marriage of the Lamb has come and His wife has made herself ready. However, the "has come" is fully realized in the new heaven and the new earth. In Revelation 21:2, John actually saw the New Jerusalem coming down from God out of heaven. At that time the bride was truly ready in every sense. This is not merely the readiness declared in chapter nineteen, but the readiness in actual fact.

Now we must turn back to read Ephesians 5:26 and 27. "That He might sanctify her, cleansing her by the washing of the water in the word, that He might present the church to Himself glorious, not having spot or wrinkle or any such things, but that she would be holy and without blemish." "That He might present the church to Himself" is fulfilled in Revelation 21. Now, before God, the bride is ready to be presented to the Lord. "Prepared as a bride" is no longer difficult to comprehend. By the end of the kingdom age, the whole church will be brought to this place. What we fail to see today will be fully seen in that day. Today we may say that God's standard for the church is high and ask how the church will ever attain to such a condition. We may not know how God will do it, but we do know that the church will attain to that position at the time of the new heaven and new earth. Some may think that the church will reach the stage of Ephesians 5 before the age of the kingdom. However, the Lord did not say this. The church will not arrive at that place until Revelation 21. At the time of the new heaven and new earth, there will not be just a group of saints who are perfected, but all the saints, the whole Body, from all the nations throughout all the ages. They will all be together before God and glorified in His presence.

Revelation 21:3 says, "And I heard a loud voice out of the throne, saying, Behold, the tabernacle of God is with men, and He will tabernacle with them, and they will be His peoples, and God Himself will be with them and be their God." This verse reveals what it will be like in the new heaven and new earth. The new heaven and new earth are in the eternal blessing, and positive blessing is spoken of here. This verse is followed by statements that say there will be no more of this and no more of that. These are the negative aspects, not the positive aspects. What is the positive and eternal blessing? It is that God will be with us. The presence of God is the blessing. All that the Scriptures have ever said about the blessing in eternity is summed up in these words, "God Himself will be with them." The severest suffering is to be without God's presence. But all of the enjoyment in eternity will be God's presence. The blessing of that day, is nothing other than God being with us. Solomon once said, "Behold, the heaven and heaven of heavens cannot contain thee; how much less this house that I have builded?" (1 Kings 8:27). The heaven and the heaven of heavens cannot contain Him, but we may say that the New Jerusalem can contain Him. God dwells in the New Jerusalem, and God's throne is established there.

The New Jerusalem is the woman whom we have been considering. In Genesis we saw a garden and a woman. This woman sinned, and God drove her out of the garden. Now in the new heaven and new earth, the woman and the holy city are one; they are no longer two separate entities. Since the New Jerusalem is the woman, the New Jerusalem is the wife of the Lamb; therefore, the woman and the holy city are one. Not only so, but God's throne is established in the New Jerusalem, or we may say that God Himself dwells within this woman. The Almighty One is dwelling in her. Therefore, it does not matter how great the force or temptation that can come from without. Evil powers can no longer enter, nor can man fall again, because God dwells within her. The blessing of the new heaven and new earth is the presence of God. All who have tasted something of God's presence in their experience know that it is indeed a blessing. No other blessing is greater or more precious than this.

Let us read again the last part of verse 3: "He will tabernacle with them, and they will be His peoples, and God Himself will be with them and be their God." Do we see the relationship between God and man? What does it really mean for us to be the people of God? It means that God will dwell with us, and therefore, we will be made His people. What does it mean that God will be our God? It means that God will be with us, and therefore, He will be our God. When we are away from His presence, God cannot be our God. The greatest and highest blessing in eternity is that God will be with us and be our God.

Verse 4 says, "And He will wipe away every tear from their eyes; and death will be no more, nor will there be sorrow or crying or pain anymore; for the former things have passed away." All men have experienced the shedding of tears, but in the new heaven and new earth they will receive this blessing—God will wipe away every tear from their eyes. Death is wholly a consequence of the fall. But in the new heaven and new earth, there will no longer be any death. The last enemy will be abolished. Sorrow or mourning is the aching of our heart, the feeling of inward suffering; crying is the weeping without, the outward expression. Pain is the suffering of our physical body. But God will put an end to all of these things. They are all summed up in the words: *every tear, death, sorrow, crying,* and *pain.* But they will be no more; they will all pass away.

Verse 5 says, "And He who sits on the throne said, Behold, I make all things new." The difficulty that we face today is that even though we are the new creation, we still live in the old creation. But in that day all things will become new; all things will be in the new creation. Not only will the inward being be new, but the outward will be as well. The entire environment and all things within it will be made new. This is called eternity. The new creation is for us. Our hearts will be satisfied only when all things are in the new creation. Isaiah 6 speaks of a painful experience which we all share: "I am a man of unclean lips." In addition, another painful experience is recorded: "And in the midst of a people of unclean lips I dwell." But in that day, everything around us will be in the new creation. That day will be absolutely glorious.

Revelation 21:5 continues, "And He said, Write, for these words are faithful and true." How good it is to have this written down. God gave these words to John and asked him to write them down. Not one iota or one serif of what is written can pass away. These words are faithful and true! Our ultimate faith will be to see God win the final victory.

In verse 6, God told John, "They have come to pass." On what ground could God say to John that it is done? He can say this because He is "the Alpha and the Omega, the Beginning and the End." It often seems that God's work has not been successful, but He says, "I am the Alpha and the Omega." God made the original design, and God also will bring it to its final completion. How we thank God that He is the Alpha, the initiator of all things. Genesis 1:1 says, "In the beginning God..." When the heavens and the earth were created, God purposed all things. All things had their beginning in God. At the same time, He is also the Omega. Man can and will fail, but God is the Omega. Man may say this and man may say that, but God has the last word. He is the Omega.

God spoke these things because He wants to tell us that He will bring His plan to fulfillment, He will reach His goal, and He will accomplish what He has begun. We acknowledge that Satan's work has indeed interrupted the work of God, but we further acknowledge that God is not only the Alpha who purposed in the beginning, but also the Omega who will finally succeed. God never gives up, and He will never let any of His purpose remain unfulfilled. Regardless of the church's condition in her present experience, she will have no spot, wrinkle, or any such things in God's goal. Furthermore, she will be clothed with glory and presented to His Son.

When we see God's children differing so much with each other in faith and doctrine as well as in practice, we wonder how it is possible for them to ever come to the oneness of the faith, as spoken of in Ephesians 4. We often sigh and say that this could never happen, even if we waited for another two thousand years. But God said that He is the Omega. The day will come when He will have a glorious church before Him. He may use water or He may use fire, but He will certainly have a glorious church. We cannot hinder God. He will obtain that which will satisfy Him. No matter how weak, how indifferent, or how hardened we are, there will be a day when God will smash us to pieces. He will break us and shatter us so that we will become what He desires us to be. God is the Omega. Since God is doing it, He will pursue it to the end. He will never let up. Let us praise Him with rejoicing. He must attain His goal!

Verse 6 continues, "I will give to him who thirsts from the spring of the water of life freely." The emphasis here is not upon redemption but upon our need for God. The meaning of thirst is a need for God. To be without God means that we are without water. Therefore, the fountain of the water of life is for the satisfaction of those who are thirsty.

Now we must pay close attention to verse 7. How we thank God for the especially precious promise in this verse, telling us what the overcomers will obtain. The overcomers spoken of here are different from those mentioned in Revelation 2 and 3. The overcomers in chapters two and three are a group from the whole church, while the overcomers spoken of here are connected with "him who thirsts." The preceding verse says, "I will give to him who thirsts from the spring of the water of life freely." Then verse 7 says, "He who overcomes will inherit these things." In other words, those who drink of the fountain of the water of life are the overcomers spoken of here. These overcomers differ from those who do not drink of this water. This kind of overcoming is the same as that which is spoken of in 1 John 5:4: "For everything that has been begotten of God overcomes the world; and this is the victory which has overcome the world—our faith." Those who are begotten of God, those who belong to the Lord, have faith. Those who do not belong to the Lord do not have faith. And this faith causes us to overcome the world. This surely should make us glad and make us rejoice and shout, Hallelujah! In the new heaven and new earth we are all overcomers! The man-child in the age of the kingdom is constituted of a minority, but in the New Jerusalem, the entire Body overcomes. In the New Jerusalem it is only a matter of whether or not we have faith. If we have faith, we are an overcomer.

In that day God will wipe away every tear from our eyes; and death will be no more, neither will there be sorrow, crying, or pain anymore, for the former things have passed away. But all these things are negative aspects. The positive is that "He will tabernacle with them, and they will be His peoples." In verse 7 God also says, "I will be God to him, and he will be a son to Me." Therefore, our position before God as Christians is not only as people, but as sons. God wants to have many sons enter into glory. We thank and praise God that He said, "I will be God to him, and he will be a son to Me." There is no higher blessing in eternity than this.

Verse 8 says, "But the cowardly and unbelieving and abominable and murderers and fornicators and sorcerers and idolaters and all the false, their part will be in the lake which burns with fire and brimstone, which is the second death." Just as the blessing in eternity is a fact, so the punishment in eternity is also a fact. The punishment from the God of love is unavoidable and inescapable. This is a severe warning to everyone.

THE HOLY CITY DESCENDING FROM HEAVEN

Now let us see the details of the holy city, the New Jerusalem. Revelation 21:9-10 says, "And one of the seven angels who had the seven bowls full of the seven last plagues came and spoke with me, saying, Come here; I will show you the bride, the wife of the Lamb. And he carried me away in spirit onto a great and high mountain and showed me the holy city, Jerusalem, coming down out of heaven from God."

When the angel wanted to show John the great harlot in Revelation 17:1-3, he led him into the wilderness. In God's eyes and in the eyes of those who are inspired by the Holy Spirit, the harlot is one who dwells in the wilderness. She lives in a place where there is no life and no fruit—a barren land. Men today can behold high church buildings, they can take part in well-prepared Sunday services, and they can admire the ability of man, but in the sight of God, everything that has its origin in Babylon is in the wilderness; it is deserted.

When the angel showed John the wife of the Lamb, he brought him up to a great and high mountain. There he showed him the holy city, Jerusalem, coming down out of heaven from God. It was from a great and high mountain that John beheld this sight. This reveals that if we desire to see the eternal vision of God, we must be brought by Him to a great and high mountain. If we are not standing spiritually on a high mountain, we will not see those who are living on the plain, we will not see the New Jerusalem, nor will we see the ultimate work of God. When Moses reached the Jordan with the children of Israel, what did God tell him to do? He commanded him to go up to the top of Mount Pisgah and lift up his eyes to behold the land which He had promised. This also tells us that in order to receive vision and revelation and to behold the plan of God, we must be upon the height.

Never think that just being an ordinary Christian day by day, not committing any great sin, is good enough. We must realize that whenever we take this position, God's eternal plan is nothing more to us than doctrine and knowledge. We must hope to do some spiritual climbing and have some spiritual attainment. We should expect to climb a high mountain. Only when we do this will we be able to see the New Jerusalem.

What God desires to do, He will accomplish. What God has purposed in eternity past, He will obtain in eternity future. First, there must be overcomers to bring in the kingdom, and then there must be overcomers to bring in the new heaven and new earth. But the problem is, who will be the overcomers? To be an overcomer, we must have revelation. If there is no revelation, it is easy to receive anything as a teaching. But we must remember that knowledge can never produce fruit; only revelation is fruitful. However, in order to have revelation we must go up to the high mountain; we cannot dwell in the plain. There is some difficulty in climbing a mountain because we must exercise our strength to climb. We cannot reach the peak unless we make some effort. May God grant us this spiritual attainment and deliver us from the low plain. We should not think that just being saved and not wanting anything more is enough. God must save us from this low level of living and show us His heart's desire. Only when we are on the high mountain will we receive revelation.

After John saw the New Jerusalem, he did a very foolish thing—he fell down to worship before the feet of the angel. This action of his, though foolish, is quite meaningful. John was the last among the twelve disciples to leave this world. His knowledge, his deeds, his love, and his experience were far beyond ours; yet in the book of Revelation, we see that he did this foolish thing twice. There were two instances in which he wanted to worship the angels—once in 19:10 and again in 22:8. Although this act of John's was unlawful and he was told, "Do not do this," yet it still reveals what a wholehearted person John was and how greatly he appreciated God's plan and work. In such a situation he was not able to restrain himself; he did something foolishly. His deed was wrong, but his heart was revealed to be right. This shows us the attitude we should have when we see God's vision. May the Lord also grant us to see such a vision. May He enable us to go up to the height to see the New Jerusalem. Oh, that everything within us would be for the success of this vision and for nothing else!

The angel said to John, "I will show you the bride, the wife of the Lamb" (21:9). The angel said that he would show him the wife of the Lamb, but John saw "the holy city, Jerusalem, coming down out of heaven from God" (v. 10). The wife of the Lamb whom John saw was the holy city, Jerusalem. Therefore, the description of the city is also the description of the wife of the Lamb. The city is a figure, describing the characteristics and spiritual condition of the corporate Body whom God chose before creation.

This city comes down out of heaven from God. This means that God not only is concerned about the destination of this corporate man, but also about the place from which this corporate man comes. It is not just a matter of the future, but a matter of the source. The wife of the Lamb comes down out of heaven. The New Jerusalem is from heaven, not from earth. God is not showing us a man with a history of sin, who was later saved. (This is not to say that we do not have a history of sin and that we do not need to repent and be saved by grace.) Rather, this passage shows us only that portion which is out from God. It shows us the glorious church of Ephesians 5 which is to be presented to Christ.

In the Old Testament, one woman represents in a special way the church which is to be offered to Christ. She is Rebecca. Abraham said to his old servant, "Thou shalt not take a wife unto my son of the daughters of the Canaanites, among whom I dwell: but thou shalt go unto my country, and to my kindred, and take a wife unto my son Isaac" (Gen. 24:3-4). Rebecca was not an inhabitant of the land west of the Euphrates, nor an inhabitant of the land west of the Jordan, but she was of the kindred of Isaac.

God desires to have a corporate man of the kindred of Christ. Since Christ is from heaven, the church too must come from heaven. Thus Hebrews 2:11 says, "For both He who sanctifies and those who are being sanctified are all of One, for which cause He is not ashamed to call them brothers." What are brothers? Brothers are those who have been born of the same mother and father. How we thank God that on one hand we were purchased with the precious blood of the Lord, and on the other hand, we were truly born of God. There are two aspects to the history of every Christian: one is that we were outwardly purchased of God, and the other is that we were inwardly born of God. From the standpoint of our history with sin, we were outwardly purchased; but from the standpoint of our history apart from sin, we were born of God, for whoever is born of God cannot sin. This portion has no beginning of sin nor history of sin. The fact that the New Jerusalem comes down from God implies that the church has never been on this earth. It appears that the church is coming down to earth for the first time. This is not to say that we did not come to God as sinners, but that there is a portion in us which is from God and is entirely of God. How we must thank the Lord that the New Jerusalem descends out of heaven from God!

This city is completely different from the city recorded in chapter seventeen. That city is called the great city, and this city is called the holy city. The characteristic of Babylon is its greatness, and the characteristic of the New Jerusalem is its holiness. Among Christians there are some who are taken up with greatness, but there are some who pay attention to holiness. Those who concentrate on greatness are in the principle of Babylon, while those who pay attention to holiness are in the principle of the New Jerusalem.

What is the meaning of holiness? Since God alone is holy, anything which issues from Him must also be holy. Saying that "both He who sanctifies and those who are being sanctified are all of One" means that Christ is holy because He is of the One and that we also are holy because we also are of the One. Only those who are of the One are holy. Only that which issues from God is of value; that which comes out from God, and only that, is the New Jerusalem. Everything that is of man must be left aside. The matter of the rapture is based upon this. Why will some be left out? It is because they have so many things which are not of Christ, and anything that is not of Christ cannot be brought to heaven. Nothing which is not of heaven can return to heaven. Everything that is of earth must be left on earth; while everything that is of heaven can return to heaven.

THE LIGHT OF THE HOLY CITY

Revelation 21:11 describes this city as "having the glory of God. Her light was like a most precious stone, like a jasper stone, as clear as crystal." Jasper has been already mentioned in Revelation 4. John saw One sitting upon the throne whose appearance was like a jasper and sardius. The One whom John saw sitting upon the throne was the same as jasper. In other words, the meaning of jasper is God seen, God made visible. When man stands before the throne, God will be known to him as jasper. This is how we will recognize Him when we go there, but not while we are here. What we realize today is quite obscure in many areas, but in that city the glory of God has the brightness of jasper. This means that when the New Jerusalem descends to earth we will be able to see God Himself. We shall never again misunderstand Him, nor will we ever need to ask the reason for anything. The light of the New Jerusalem is as clear as crystal, without a trace of mixture. In that day, everything will be transparent and clearly shown to us. In that day we will see God, and we will know God.

THE INHABITANTS OF THE HOLY CITY

Verses 12-14 say, "It had a great and high wall and had twelve gates, and at the gates twelve angels, and names inscribed, which are the names of the twelve tribes of the sons of Israel: on the east three gates, and on the north three gates, and on the south three gates, and on the west three gates. And the wall of the city had twelve foundations, and on them the twelve names of the twelve apostles of the Lamb." How many are included in this corporate man? We are told that the names of the twelve tribes of Israel are written upon the gates, and the names of the twelve apostles are written upon the foundations. This shows us that the city includes the saints from both the Old and the New Testament.

This can be proved by reading the following passages of Scripture. Luke 13:28-29 says, "There will be weeping and gnashing of teeth there when you see Abraham and Isaac and Jacob and all the prophets in the kingdom of God, but you being cast outside. And they will come from the east and the west, and from the north and the south, and will recline at table in the kingdom of God." Here we see that the kingdom of God includes Abraham, Isaac, and Jacob, who represent the Old Testament saints. Those who come from the east, west, north, and south represent the New Testament saints. These two groups of people are participants in the kingdom of God; therefore, they will all enter into the New Jerusalem together.

Hebrews 11:8-10 says, "By faith Abraham...dwelt as a foreigner in the land of promise as in a foreign land, making his home in tents with Isaac and Jacob, the fellow heirs of the same promise; for he eagerly waited for the city which has the foundations, whose Architect and Builder is God." The city referred to in this passage is the New Jerusalem. Only this city is a city with foundations, whose Architect and Builder is God. Verse 13 says, "All these died in faith." "All these" are Abel, Enoch, Noah, Abraham, Isaac, Jacob, and many others. Verse 16 continues, "But as it is, they long after a better country, that is, a heavenly one. Therefore God is not ashamed of them, to be called their God, for He has prepared a city for them." "They" in verse 16 are the "these" in verse 13. This shows us that the Old Testament saints have a portion in the New Jerusalem. From Abel at the beginning and for all the saints in the Old Testament, God has appointed a city, the New Jerusalem. They all have their share in it. Verses 39-40 say, "And these all, having obtained a good testimony through their faith, did not obtain the promise, because God has provided something better for us, so that apart from us they would not be made perfect." God has kept all the Old Testament saints waiting; they have not yet obtained that city. He has bid them to wait so that both we and they might go there together. From this we see that both the saints of the Old Testament and the saints of the New Testament will be in the New Jerusalem.

Ephesians 2:11-14 says, "Therefore remember that once you, the Gentiles in the flesh, those who are called uncircumcision,...that you were at that time apart from Christ, alienated from the commonwealth of Israel, and strangers to the covenants of the promise, having no hope and without God in the world. But now in Christ Jesus you who were once far off have become near in the blood of Christ. For He Himself is our peace, He who has made both one and has broken down the middle wall of partition." From verse 11 to 13, the pronoun "you" is used, but in verse 14, it changes to "our." When "you" is used, it refers to the saints in Ephesus, but when "our" is used, it refers both to the Jewish saints and the Ephesian saints as well as all the saints of both the Old and New Testaments. Christ is our peace and He has made both one, breaking down the middle wall of partition. Verse 15 says, "Abolishing in His flesh the law of the commandments in ordinances, that He might create the two in Himself into one new man, so making peace." The "two" in this verse corresponds with the "both" in verse 14. This also refers to Old Testament saints as well as New Testament saints. It does not refer to the relationship between man and God. Could God and man be created together to become a new man? No. This passage refers to both the saints of the Gentiles and the saints of the Jews, the Old Testament saints as well as the New Testament saints.

Verse 16 says, "And might reconcile both in one Body to God through the cross, having slain the enmity by it." To reconcile "both in one Body" to God means that the Old Testament saints as well as the New Testament saints are reconciled to God. Verses 17-19 say, "And coming, He announced peace as the gospel to you who were far off, and peace to those who were near, for through Him we both have access in one Spirit unto the Father. So then you are no longer strangers and sojourners, but you are fellow citizens with the saints and members of the household of God." The saints in Ephesus were no longer strangers but fellow citizens with the saints and members of the household of God. Verses 20-22 say, "Being built upon the foundation of the apostles and prophets, Christ Jesus Himself being the cornerstone; in whom all the building, being fitted together, is growing into a holy temple in the Lord; in whom you also are being built together into a dwelling place of God in spirit." Thus, the habitation of God includes all the saints of the Old and New Testament. Abraham, Isaac, and Jacob are there, and we also are there. In conclusion, at the time of the new heaven and new earth, all those who have the life of God will be included in the New Jerusalem.

THE CITY, THE GATES, AND THE WALL

Let us continue in our reading of Revelation 21. We must give special attention to the wall of the city. Verse 12 says, "It had a great and high wall." Verse 15 says, "He who spoke with me had a golden reed as a measure that he might measure the city and its gates and its wall." Verse 17 says, "And he measured its wall, a hundred and forty-four cubits, according to the measure of a man, that is, of an angel."

In the beginning God made a garden in Eden, and the serpent was able to come into this garden to speak to Eve. This shows us that there was no wall surrounding the garden. God originally intended for Adam to keep the garden. In other words, His intention was that Adam would be the wall of the garden. However, Adam did not guard it, and Satan entered. But what about the New Jerusalem? The New Jerusalem has a wall. On one hand, a wall includes, and on the other hand, it excludes. It includes and keeps everything that is within the city, and it excludes and rejects everything that is outside the city. When there is a wall surrounding a city, it serves to separate everything that is within the city from everything that is outside; it serves to make a difference between them. The New Jerusalem is the new man whom God has desired to obtain. The new man is in God's presence and separated from all that is outside. The serpent can no longer creep in. There is a wall, a separation, a distinction. Every possibility of the serpent entering again has been eliminated.

When describing the New Jerusalem, the first thing that is mentioned other than God's glory is the wall. Separation, therefore, is one of the most important principles in a Christian's living. If there is no separation, the Christian is of no value. There must be a line that is drawn to differentiate that which is spiritual from that which is fleshly. The New Jerusalem has a separation, a boundary line, and we need to learn a lesson from this. Everything that is of Babylon must be rejected, while everything that is of God must be protected. To build a city wall is not an easy thing, because Satan hates a wall more than anything else. When Nehemiah returned to Jerusalem to build the wall, Sanballat and Tobiah came and made every effort to stop the building. Nehemiah held a spear in one hand, and with the other hand, he built the wall. We must pray, therefore, that God will enable us to bear spiritual arms in order to wrestle with spiritual wickedness in high places and in order to maintain the principle of separation.

The city has twelve gates and twelve foundations, and on the foundations are the names of the twelve apostles of the Lamb. This tells us that everything in the city is based upon the principles of the kingdom of God preached by the apostles. Ephesians 2:20 says, "Being built upon the foundation of the apostles and prophets." This means that the revelation which the apostles obtained is the foundation of the New Jerusalem.

The gates are for going in and out, but why are the names of the twelve tribes of Israel written upon them? The Lord Jesus said that salvation is of the Jews (John 4:22). We have learned everything related to God from Israel. The law was given to Israel, redemption is known through Israel, and salvation has come from Israel. Therefore, the names of the twelve tribes of Israel are on the gates.

The city has three gates on the east, three gates on the north, three gates on the south, and three gates on the west. There are three gates in each direction. Gates are usually located in a convenient place to go in and out. Therefore, the fact that this city has gates on all four sides indicates that it is located in a very central position and that it is the center of everything. The New Jerusalem is the masterpiece in the center of God's heart.

Praise God. At the gates there are twelve angels to keep the entrance (Rev. 21:12). Formerly cherubim guarded the way of the tree of life, but now the tree of life in the city is guarded by angels at the gates. The angels are ministering spirits (Heb. 1:14), and the day is coming when angels will be subject to the church.

Revelation 21:15 says, "And he who spoke with me had a golden reed as a measure that he might measure the city and its gates and its wall." Gold in the Bible represents all that is of God. The city being measured with gold means that the city can be measured by God's standard and corresponds with God's standard. We need to seek God's glory, hoping that we will be able to meet God's standard when we are measured in that day.

Verse 16 says, "And the city lies square, and its length is as great as the breadth. And he measured the city with the reed to a length of twelve thousand stadia; the length and the breadth and the height of it are equal." There is another place in the Bible where the measurements of length, breadth, and height are equal, that is the Holy of Holies in the temple. "And the oracle in the forepart was twenty cubits in length, and twenty cubits in breadth, and twenty cubits in the height thereof" (1 Kings 6:20). The length, the breadth, and the height are all the same. In the Bible, only the Holy of Holies in the temple and the city of the New Jerusalem have equal measurements of length, breadth, and height. In other words, in the new heaven and new earth, the New Jerusalem becomes the Holy of Holies to God. When David gave Solomon the pattern for the temple, he said, "All this...the Lord made me understand in writing by his hand upon me, even all the works of this pattern" (1 Chron. 28:19). Everything in the temple was built according to divine revelation. In the new heaven and new earth, the New Jerusalem is the very temple of God. Everything that constitutes the city is something in God. There is nothing that is outside of Him.

Revelation 21:17 says, "And he measured its wall, a hundred and forty-four cubits, according to the measure of a man, that is, of an angel." Today can we say that the measure of a man is that of an angel? No, never. At what time will the measure of a man be equal to that of an angel? The Lord Jesus said that in the resurrection man will be equal to the angels (Luke 20:36). The one hundred and forty-four cubits will be revealed when man's measure is equal to an angel's measure. In other words, everything within this city is in the reality of resurrection. Thank God, of all the things included in this city, there is nothing which is not in resurrection. Everything that is dead and everything that is of man is outside the city, but inside everything is resurrected and of God. Resurrection means that which is of God. Everything that is of man, once it dies, can never be raised up, but everything that is of God, though it passes through death, will rise again. Whatever cannot be bound or held by death is called resurrection. When that which originates from us passes through the cross, it is brought to an end, but nothing of God can be touched by death.

When John recorded the description of the city, all the numbers he used were *twelve* or products of twelve—twelve gates, twelve foundations, twelve apostles, twelve tribes, etc. The measurement of the city wall is one hundred and forty-four cubits, the product of twelve times twelve. Twelve is the number used in eternity. It is the most precious number in the Bible. In the first part of Revelation, there are many sevens—seven churches, seven seals, seven trumpets, seven bowls, seven angels, etc. But in the latter part, there are many twelves, such as those already mentioned. Seven means perfection, and twelve also means perfection, but they are not altogether the same. Seven is composed of three plus four, while twelve is composed of three multiplied by four. Since God is the Triune God, the number three represents God, while four is the number which represents creation, such as the four winds, the four seasons, and the four living creatures. When three is added to four, it means that God is added to man. How complete and perfect it is to have the Creator plus the creature! But anything which is added can also be subtracted and thereby lost again; so this completion is not a lasting one. But in the New Jerusalem, the union of God and man is no longer seven, but twelve. It is no longer three plus four, but three multiplied by four. Multiplication is a perfect union, something which can never be separated. When the Creator mingles with the creature it is twelve, and twelve is the number of perfect union. In the new heaven and new earth, God and man will become one, and God and man can no longer be separated.

GOLD, PRECIOUS STONES, AND PEARL

Of what materials is this city built? Verse 18 says, "And the building work of its wall was jasper." We have noted jasper already. We have seen that the brightness of the city is as jasper. The meaning of this is that when we behold the glory of the city we are looking at God's real image. By knowing God's real image, man can know the God who is

sitting upon the throne. God is not far away from man, nor is
He an unknowable God.

The function of the city wall, as we have seen, is to separate that which is within the city from that which is without.
The fact that this wall is made of jasper means that the separation is based upon what is seen in God's true light. The
basis of separation is the seeing of what God requires, the
seeing of what God is after. If man is not clear about God's
requirement, he will have no separation.

Let us read further in verse 18: "And the city was pure
gold, like clear glass." In other words, all that is in the city
is of God. Gold signifies that which is of God, that which is
placed in God's new creation. Peter said that we are partak-
ers of the divine nature. Within everyone who belongs to God,
there is a portion which is of God. Before we were saved,
everything in us was of the flesh, everything was natural;
there was nothing whatever of a spiritual nature. But when
we received the Lord, God imparted His life to us. This is
the gold which He has given us. Within us there is a portion
of gold; there is something which is truly of God. It is regret-
table, however, that although we have this gold in us, it is
mixed with many other things; it is an alloy. We have God's
nature, but at the same time, we also have many things in us
which are completely different from God. For this reason, the
greater portion of God's work with His children is to reduce
them, not to add to them.

Many times men would like to obtain more of God, to be
filled with the Holy Spirit, and to know Christ better. All of
these things have their place. We dearly need to obtain more
of God, to be filled with the Spirit, and to know more of
Christ. But there is another work—it is not of increasing but
of reducing. God's basic work is to reduce us. From the day
we were saved, God has been doing this work, and the instrument for this work of subtraction is the cross. The work of the
cross is to cancel out. It is not to bring things into us but to
take things away from us. Within us there is so much that is
refuse. There are so many things that are not of God, which
do not bring glory to Him. God wants to remove all of these
things through the cross so that we may become pure gold.

What God has put into us is pure gold, but because there is so much dross in us, so many things which are not of God, we have become an alloy. Therefore, God must expend much effort to make us see those things in us which are of self and those things which cannot bring glory to Him. We believe that if God speaks to us, we will discover that what needs to be removed is much more than what needs to be added. Christians who are especially strong in the soul must remember that God's work in them through the Holy Spirit is to remove things from them and to reduce them.

The outstanding feature of the New Jerusalem is that of gold, pure gold. There is nothing there which contains a mixture; everything is entirely of God. The one lesson which God wants us to learn today is to see that everything coming from us is but dross. Apart from the gold in us, everything which comes from us is refuse. When added to the gold, our goodness is dross; when added to the gold, our zeal is also dross. Everything from us is dross. In other words, anything which is not of God is dross. No one can stand before God and say that he has something to contribute to Him. God demands pure gold. In the New Jerusalem everything is pure gold, without any dross. The day will come when we see that everything that is not of God is on the cross. Everything that is in the New Jerusalem is of God. God must attain His purpose. When God says that it will be pure gold, it will be pure gold. There is nothing which can be mixed with God's work.

Verses 19 and 20 say, "The foundations of the wall of the city were adorned with every precious stone: the first foundation was jasper; the second, sapphire; the third, chalcedony; the fourth, emerald; the fifth, sardonyx; the sixth, sardius; the seventh, chrysolite; the eighth, beryl; the ninth, topaz; the tenth, chrysoprase; the eleventh, jacinth; the twelfth, amethyst." What do precious stones imply? There is a basic difference between precious stones and gold. Gold is a chemical element, while a precious stone is not a chemical element, but a compound. Gold is an element because God created it as gold; it was made directly by God. But a precious stone has been formed from various kinds of elements, which have been composed together through chemical combination through countless years of heat and pressure in the earth. In other words, the precious stones do not signify something given directly by God, but something which the Holy Spirit has produced in man by much effort and many years of burning. The work of the Holy Spirit on earth is to continually put us into trials so that we may have all kinds of experiences and become precious stones before Him. The precious stones, therefore, are the product of our being disciplined by Him.

Let us illustrate. Isaac's birth represents gold, but Jacob's experience represents precious stone. Isaac was born a son through the promise of God. He never suffered, nor was he ever seriously at fault. Jacob's case, however, was quite different. He suffered very much and passed through many trials. God's hand was upon him all the time. Day after day and year after year, God wrought something into Jacob which caused him to become a precious stone.

That life which God has imparted to us is the gold, while the life which God is constituting in us is the precious stone. Day after day, in all kinds of circumstances, He is making us in the image of Christ. This is the precious stone. God does not stop by just giving us a portion of Christ's life; He wants to have the life of Christ wrought into us. On one hand, we must realize that except for the Lord's life in us we are not any different than we were prior to our salvation. But on the other hand, after following the Lord for five or ten years and being disciplined and dealt with by Him, a portion of the life of Christ has been constituted in us by the Holy Spirit. There is something within us which has been formed by the Lord, and this is the precious stone.

You should not be surprised when God continually puts you into the fire to burn. It seems that the things which other people encounter are all good, but the things which you are up against are not prosperous or easy. You are even misunderstood and attacked by others; more things have happened to you than to anyone else. But you must realize that it is not without a cause. God is continually burning you; the Holy Spirit is working to constitute more of the life of Christ in you so that you may be transformed into His image.

In Revelation we find not just one kind of precious stone, but all kinds of precious stones. Some are jasper, some sapphire, some chalcedony, some emerald, some sardonyx, some sardius, and other kinds. All of these precious stones are the product of burning. They were not formed by God in a moment of time but obtained after being wrought upon through long years of God's working. Precious stone was not given to us at creation, nor is it something we obtained when we became a new creation. Precious stone is formed in us through God's burning day after day. It is a substance which is constantly put into the fire. When the fire burns in a certain way, a certain kind of mineral is melted into that substance, and it becomes a certain kind of precious stone. When the fire burns in another way, it causes another kind of mineral to be dissolved into that substance, causing it to become another kind of precious stone. Different ways of melting certain minerals together form various kinds of precious stones.

The precious stones represent the work of the Holy Spirit. When we were saved we obtained God's nature, but from that time, day after day, the Holy Spirit has been working the nature of God into us so that we may bear the fruit of the Spirit. There is not just one fruit of the Spirit. There are love, joy, peace, longsuffering, kindness, goodness, faithfulness, meekness, and many others. The Holy Spirit must continually work in us to cause us to bear all these different kinds of fruit. When we were saved, God imparted His life into us. But the fruit of the Spirit is not something imparted to us by God. We bear these fruits when the Holy Spirit works within us to a certain extent. Even so, precious stone is something formed in us through the Holy Spirit by means of many different circumstances.

Not only has God shared His nature with us, but day by day He is making us a certain kind of people who can bring glory to His name. When you were saved, you obtained God's nature, and when I was saved, I obtained His nature. In this regard, all Christians are the same; they all have obtained God's nature. But in the ensuing days, God may have put you into certain circumstances in order to give you certain kinds of experience. He may have let you go through certain trials, certain difficulties, and certain sufferings so that you will become a Christian like chrysolite, chalcedony, sardius, or some other precious stone. God is working in every Christian so that each one may become a certain kind of precious stone. We all have gold in common before God, but after we become precious stones before Him, we will each be a certain form.

What the Holy Spirit forms in us by means of the environment will abide forever. When a Christian receives more dealings in a certain way, he will learn more lessons in that way. This will produce an outstanding character in him, a character which will not come to an end after several years, but which will abide for eternity. What he has obtained will forever be a precious stone in the New Jerusalem.

In many of God's children who have walked with Him for ten or twenty years, there is something which God has wrought through the Holy Spirit. It is not just that God has imparted something to them, but they themselves have become that something; it is their very constituent. They have been disciplined by the Holy Spirit for many years. By passing through many trials and experiences, the Holy Spirit has formed a certain kind of life in them. Those who are acquainted with them acknowledge that something has indeed been accomplished in them. They not only possess the life that is given to them by God, but they also have a transformed life which the Holy Spirit has wrought within them. Not only do they live an exchanged life but also a transformed life. This is the precious stone. Precious stone is that which has been formed in us by the burning work of the Holy Spirit. The New Jerusalem will be filled with these precious stones.

At this point we must realize how useless it is to put our emphasis merely on doctrine. We must never think that we will benefit if we only know a little more theology or scriptural teaching. These are not of much use. Only that which is burned into us by the Holy Spirit is of value. If something has not been burned into an article, a little rubbing will remove it. What spiritual value is there in something which can be wiped away from us with a little rubbing? This does not mean that we should not read our Bible, but it does mean that what we read is of value only when the Holy Spirit burns it into us. All precious stones have come out of fire. To have precious stones, we need the fire. Without fire, there will never be any precious stone.

For this reason we should never refuse the trials that come upon us through our environment. We should never refuse the discipline of the Holy Spirit, nor complain when God's hand encircles and encloses us in every way. How bound and pressed we feel many times! How we would like to break through all the bondage and limitation and be released for a while. But we must remember that we are in God's forming hand. He is forming us so that one day we will come out as precious stones. God has not only given us His life, but He is also working in us to the extent that we may possess a special quality. This is what the Holy Spirit is forming in us through all the circumstances which God allows, and this is called precious stone. What use is it then to merely have knowledge or doctrine? Only that which the Spirit burns into us is of any value. Only when a Christian has received something through burning will he be able to preach messages from what he really knows rather than from books. Only that which has been burned into us by the Holy Spirit is precious stone. Otherwise, it is wood, grass, and stubble.

Sometimes when we sit in the presence of an elderly person, we feel that he is one who is really walking with the Lord. There is a life in him which very much characterizes him; it has become his special nature. We can only bow down before him. There may be others who have a greater ministry than he and others who have undertaken a greater work, but he has an abundant life; something has been formed within him by the Holy Spirit. He has a special quality, something which has come out from the fire; he is a precious stone. In the presence of such a one we can only bow and say, "How we wish that we also may have something that is so inspiring, so touching." It is not words which inspire and touch people, but something which has gone through the fire.

In the New Jerusalem there are precious stones. Without precious stones, the New Jerusalem will never come into existence. God needs precious stones. He needs a group of people who will manifest the quality of precious stones. Oh, may God deliver us from being shallow! Only what the Holy Spirit has wrought into our life is of any value or use.

Verse 21 continues, "And the twelve gates were twelve pearls; each one of the gates was, respectively, of one pearl." The New Jerusalem consists not only of pure gold and precious stones, but also of pearls. Pearls are not formed by burning; they are the result of a gradual formation within a sea creature after it has been wounded. Therefore, the meaning of pearl is life which issues from death. Pearl signifies the life released by the Lord Jesus in the non-redemptive aspect of His death.

Matthew 13 also speaks about a pearl. To whom does this pearl refer? It is a reference to the church, which the Lord has formed out of His death. He was willing to sell all that He had in order to purchase this pearl. Pearl signifies something positive, not something passive or negative. It is the church, the new man, that God desires to create. Within such a One there is no problem of sin, nor of redemption. He was willing to sell all to obtain this pearl. This shows us how precious is the life which is wholly out of Christ. How precious it is to God, and how precious it is to Christ!

In the New Jerusalem, pearls function as the gates of the city. This means that everything of God starts from here. In other words, in order for man to obtain life before God, the life must not be something of man, but of the death of Christ, of the non-redemptive aspect of Christ's death.

First Corinthians 3:12 says that spiritual building should have materials of gold, silver, and precious stones, not wood, grass, or stubble. In 1 Corinthians 3 there are gold, silver, and precious stones; but in Genesis 2, in the garden of Eden, there were gold, precious stones, and pearl—there was no silver. In Revelation 21, in the New Jerusalem, there are once again gold, precious stones, and pearl; there is no silver. What is the significance of this? Gold, precious stones, and pearl—these three items—are found both in the garden of

Eden and in the New Jerusalem. This means that gold, precious stones, and pearl are from eternity to eternity.

In eternity God did not plan to have silver, because silver represents redemption. God knew that men would sin and need redemption, but this was not something of His eternal plan. In God's work there is redemption, but in His eternal purpose there is no redemption. Therefore, the New Jerusalem in this respect is the same as the garden of Eden—there is no silver. This means that in eternity future, we will be brought to the place where there is no trace of sin. Today, however, we cannot disregard or lightly esteem the silver. If anyone thinks he has no need of silver today, he must ask God for mercy. We cannot go on without silver. If we have no silver, we have no redemption, and we can do nothing. But redemption has no part in God's purpose. In the New Jerusalem we will not be able to find any silver. This shows us that God will wipe away all history of sin, because redemption is not included in that city. In the New Jerusalem man will no longer need redemption, because they will sin no more. God will bring us to such a firm ground that there will be no possibility for us to fall again. There is a life within us which has nothing to do with sin and which requires no redemption. That life in us is from Christ and it is Christ Himself. As Christ Himself needs no redemption, we who have a portion of His life will no longer need redemption. Thus, in eternity there is no need of silver.

Thank God that we have His redemption today. Thank God that although we have sinned, the blood of Jesus Christ His Son cleanses us from every sin. However, God has shared the life of His Son with us, a life which forever needs no redemption. One day we will live completely by this life and the history of sin will pass away. Redeeming silver will no longer be of any use.

We must see that the fall is not in the purpose of God, redemption is not in the purpose of God, and neither is the kingdom something in the purpose of God. The fall is not in God's purpose; it is something which happened on the way. Redemption is not in God's purpose; it is the solution to the fall. And the kingdom is also not in God's purpose; it is also the solution to the fall. Because of the fall there is redemption, and because of the fall there is the kingdom. All these things are but remedies; they are not in the purpose of God. Even so, we would never make light of redemption and the kingdom. If there was no redemption, there would be no way to solve the problem of the fall. If there was no kingdom, could the matter of the fall be solved? Nevertheless, we must bear in mind that God did not create man that he might sin. God created man for His own glory. This line is straight; this heavenly line is straight.

Revelation 21:21 also says, "And the street of the city was pure gold, like transparent glass." A street is a place for communication, and since the street of this city is of pure gold, the people who walk upon it will never be dirty. Today those who have bathed still need to have their feet washed (John 13:10) in order to maintain their fellowship with God. When we walk on the street of this world, we cannot avoid gathering some dust, and our fellowship with God is thus frustrated. But in that day nothing can dirty us; nothing can frustrate our fellowship with God. In eternity there will be nothing which can defile us; all our life and living will be holy.

The end of verse 21 tells us that the city is "like transparent glass." How much of our situation today is not transparent! But in the future, in God's presence, we will all be transparent. Even so, today we should not have many hiding places and many veils. We should not pretend to be godly before men in order to win their praise. Hypocrisy, pretense, and veils—none of these are transparent. When our actual condition is not so good and we pretend to be good, we are not transparent. Many times our words and our actions are quite unnatural. We imitate others in our speaking, in our conduct, and in the way we do things. In so many ways we imitate others instead of being ourselves. This is not being transparent. All artificiality and imitation are not transparent. We certainly do not need to live before God by any self-made holiness. We must remember that real spirituality is to bear the cross. Holiness which is full of bondage is not the holiness of the Holy Spirit. All play-acting and all pretense must be abandoned.

Therefore, we need to confess many things. Among the brothers and sisters we need to learn to confess to each other and not to cover our sin. Whenever we have sinned against others, we should not try to rationalize it away, but confess it. Every Christian should be transparent today, for in that day, in the presence of God, we will all be transparent. The street in the New Jerusalem is transparent as glass. Everything is visible there. Since it will be so in that day, we must learn today to be such people—those who are real, those who are transparent, those who never act what they are not.

THE TEMPLE AND THE LIGHT OF THE CITY

Verse 22 says, "And I saw no temple in it, for the Lord God the Almighty and the Lamb are its temple." These words are especially precious. We know that in the Jerusalem of the Old Testament there was the temple. Whenever man wanted to have fellowship with God at that time, he had to go to the temple. The temple was the place set aside for God, and it was to that place that man had to go for fellowship with God. In the New Jerusalem, however, there will be no temple, because God and the Lamb are the temple of the city. This means that the fellowship between God and man in that day will be intimate and direct; it will be face to face. Man will no longer need to go to a specified place in order to have fellowship with God.

In the Old Testament there was a veil in the temple. No one could pass through this veil and enter into God's presence except the High Priest, and then only once a year. Today in the church the veil has been split. Now we all can enter into God's presence to worship Him in spirit and in truthfulness. But in that day God and the Lamb will be the temple of the city. We will not have to go to God; He will be right where we are. Today we go to God, but in that day we will live in His presence. God and the Lamb are the temple of the city. Therefore, if we do not learn to live in the Holy of Holies today, we are the most foolish people. Today the veil has been split, and we can enter into the Holy of Holies with boldness. We must not stay outside.

Verse 23 says, "And the city has no need of the sun or of the moon that they should shine in it, for the glory of God illumined it, and its lamp is the Lamb." This passage is connected with the previous verse about the temple. God and the Lamb are the temple of the city, and the glory of God lights the city. Therefore, there is no need for the sun or the moon to shine. We know that in the temple of the Old Testament the outer court was lighted by the sun and the moon, and the Holy Place by the light of the lamp. But in the Holy of Holies there was no window; the light of the sun and the moon could not shine in. Neither was there a lamp as in the Holy Place. The glory of God provided the light. Even so, the New Jerusalem is not lighted by the sun or the moon, but by the glory of God. This reveals that the whole city will be the Holy of Holies. The church in the future will become the very Holy of Holies.

"Its lamp is the Lamb." God's glory is the light and the Lamb is the lamp. This shows us that in the New Jerusalem there will still be something indirect. God as the light will shine through the Lamb as the lamp. This is not a reference to redemption but an indication to us that no one can know God directly. If anyone wants to know God, he must know Him through the Lamb—this remains true, even in eternity. Only through Christ can man know God. Apart from the lamp we cannot see the light; likewise, without Christ we cannot see God. Regardless of the environment, God still dwells in unapproachable light. Only when we are in Christ can we see Him.

Verse 24 says, "And the nations will walk by its light; and the kings of the earth bring their glory into it." We should notice one thing here. All the people whom God has obtained from the dispensation of the patriarchs, the dispensation of the law, and the dispensation of grace will become a bride to be presented to Christ in that day. All the people who are still living at the end of the age of the kingdom and who have not been deceived by Satan will be transferred to become the people on the new earth. These people are the nations mentioned in verse 24. All those who are living in the city will have resurrected bodies; they are the sons and the kings.

However, those who are on the new earth will still have a body of flesh and blood; they are the people and the nations of the earth. The kings of the earth are the rulers of the nations.

In the Old Testament the tabernacle was arranged so that it was in the center of the Israelites' camp. Three tribes dwelt on the east, three on the west, three on the south, and three on the north. This is recorded in the book of Numbers. The position of the New Jerusalem is similar to that of the tabernacle of God. The wall of this city has three gates in each direction: on the east, west, south, and north—a total of twelve gates. As the twelve tribes dwelt around the tabernacle, the nations will dwell around the New Jerusalem. The fact that the nations will "walk" by the light of the city means that the nations on earth will come to the New Jerusalem, and their walk to the New Jerusalem will be guided by the light of the city.

The "glory" which the kings shall bring refers to that glory which belongs to the kings of the earth. They will give the city the glory of their domain. "Glory" here has the same meaning as "glory" in Genesis 31:1. It means the best produce of the land. In other words, in the new earth the kings of the earth will bring the best produce of their localities and present it as a gift to the holy city.

Revelation 21:25 says, "And its gates shall by no means be shut by day, for there will be no night there." The fact that the gates will not be shut by day reveals that in the new heaven and new earth there will still be the difference between day and night. The nations can come to the city in their day time. But "there will be no night there"—in the city there will be no night. Since all those who dwell in the city will have resurrected bodies, they will never feel tired; they can serve God constantly day and night.

Verse 26 says, "And they will bring the glory and the honor of the nations into it." This refers to the kings of verse 24. The kings of the earth will not only bring their glory to the city, but they will bring the glory and the honor of the nations into it.

Verse 27 says, "And anything common and he who makes an abomination and a lie shall by no means enter into it, but only those who are written in the Lamb's book of life." Everything that is of man and everything that belongs to the flesh are common. Therefore, whatever belongs to man and the flesh cannot enter into the city. Only what is of Christ and the Holy Spirit can enter; anything else cannot get in. "He who makes an abomination" in the Scriptures especially refers to idolatry, and he who makes "a lie" refers to a relationship with Satan, because lies are from Satan. Those who are related to idols or to sin cannot enter into the city. Only those whose names are written in the Lamb's book of life can enter.

In the new heaven and new earth there will only be two kinds of inhabitants: First, there are those who have been saved by the blood—they will dwell in the city and have their names written in the book of life. Then there are those who will be transferred from the millennium—they will continue to live and become the inhabitants of the new earth. Their names are also written in the book of life, but they will not live in the city. They can only go in and come out of the city.

THE RIVER OF WATER OF LIFE AND THE TREE OF LIFE

We have yet to see what God will show us at the end. Verses 22:1-2 say, "And he showed me a river of water of life, bright as crystal, proceeding out of the throne of God and of the Lamb in the middle of its street. And on this side and on that side of the river was the tree of life, producing twelve fruits, yielding its fruit each month; and the leaves of the tree are for the healing of the nations." Here we are reminded of verse 2:7, which says, "To him who overcomes, to him I will give to eat of the tree of life, which is in the Paradise of God." The tree of life is planted in the Paradise of God. Since the tree of life is in the city, this tells us that the New Jerusalem is the Paradise of God.

Recalling the book of Genesis, God created man as a type of Christ and the woman as a type of the church he desired to obtain in Genesis 2. God then put them, husband and wife, in the garden of Eden. Thus we have the man, the woman, and the garden. Then in Genesis 3 the serpent came in and they fell; as a result, God drove them out of the garden. In

Revelation 21, whom do we see in the New Jerusalem? There is the Lamb, the One whom Adam typified in Genesis 2; He is wholly for God. There is also the wife of the Lamb, who was typified by Eve in Genesis 2; she is wholly for Christ. The New Jerusalem is the wife of the Lamb and is also the Paradise of God. In Genesis 2 there were three entities—Adam, Eve, and the garden. But in Revelation 21 and 22 there are only two—the Lamb and the city. The city is the bride and also the Paradise; the woman and the Paradise have become one. The woman in Genesis could be driven away, while the woman at the end of Revelation can no longer be driven out.

Some people may worry and ask, "What will happen in eternity? What if the devil should come in again—then what would we do?" We can answer that it is impossible for this to happen again, because in eternity God Himself will dwell in the holy city. Praise God! He set up a garden in Genesis, a garden which had no wall and which was not guarded well. Therefore, the serpent and sin could enter. But God finally obtains a city for the sake of protection. It is impossible for this city to be ever involved in a fall. The woman and Paradise have been so joined that nothing can ever separate them again. Henceforth, this woman cannot be driven out by any means.

Verse 22:1 speaks of a river of water of life being in the middle of the street of the city. In Genesis there were four rivers, two of which have always oppressed the children of God. Babylon was built upon the river Pison, and Nineveh upon the river Hiddekel. God's children have always been persecuted by these two rivers. But in the New Jerusalem there is only one river—the river of water of life. This river gives life and joy to man. Psalm 46:4 says: "There is a river whose streams gladden the city of God, / The holy place of the tabernacles of the Most High." This river especially gives gladness to God. The water of this river proceeds "out of the throne of God and of the Lamb." The throne is singular because God and the Lamb are sitting on one throne. This means that the reign of Christ is the reign of God.

Verse 2 says, "And on this side and on that side of the river was the tree of life, producing twelve fruits, yielding its fruit each month." Once again the number twelve is used. What does it mean that the tree bears twelve kinds of fruits and yields its fruit every month? This is a way of saying that everything is satisfied, and that this satisfaction is for eternity. Every month there is life. In eternity we will continue to know Christ and continue to receive the life of the Lord without any interruption—there will not be a month when there is no fruit. This means that there will be no regression. Today we see something which is very sad—that which the Scripture shows as the evaluation of man. Men from twenty years of age to sixty years of age were given a certain valuation, but the value was lowered for those over sixty years of age (Lev. 27:3, 7). This is going backward, but in eternity there will be no going backward. There will be new life and new fruit every month.

Even so, before the New Jerusalem comes into being, we need to seek a new experience of life every month. The particular experience we had twenty years ago is no longer fresh, nor can it be of any help to us today. Neither can the experience of five years ago be fresh or of any profit to us now. We cannot live by the fruit of the tree of life from former months. Each month we must continue to have fresh fruit. Before God we must receive life continuously; we must receive Christ. Not only do we need fruit each month, we need a different kind of fruit each month. We cannot be satisfied before God only having a little portion, a certain part. We must learn to know the Lord in many aspects; we must bear all manner of fruits.

Verse 2 continues, "And the leaves of the tree are for the healing of the nations." Fruit represents life; leaves, the clothing of the tree, represent our external behavior. The Lord Jesus cursed the fig tree because it only had leaves; there was no fruit. It only had the outward behavior without the inward life. In the new heaven and new earth, the people of the nations will have no sin, no death, no pain, no curse, nor any demons. This group of people, the nations, will continue living in the earth with the holy city in their midst. Being healed by the leaves of the Lord Jesus means that the deeds of the Lord Jesus will be their example. We will obtain the fruits of the tree of life, and they will obtain the leaves. By following the behavior of the Lord Jesus, they will be able to live on in well-being; and this way the nations will dwell together in peace and blessing.

In these verses the street, the river of water of life, and the tree of life are all linked together. In the New Jerusalem, wherever you find the street, you will find the river of water of life, and wherever you find the river of water of life, you will find the tree of life. In other words, wherever there is activity, there will be the river of life and the tree of life. This means that as we learn to follow the Lord, all our conduct should include the river of water of life and the tree of life. Then everything will be well. The street is a place for people to move about. In order to move about we need to have all of our activities based upon the tree of life, not upon the tree of the knowledge of good and evil. When the life within us generates the activity, the result will be the outflow of the river of the water of life in the Spirit. The outflowing of life is our street, our way. If the life of the Lord Jesus is not moving in us, we simply cannot walk. If there is not the life of the Lord and if there is not the outflow of the river of water of life in the Spirit, we cannot move. If, according to our own wisdom, we judge whether a certain way to act is good or bad, we are planting the tree of the knowledge of good and evil, not the tree of life. But if we act according to the moving of the life within, the result will be that the water of life will flow out to others. All of these things are linked together. All of God's work is based upon the tree of life and results in the river of water of life.

FOREVER AND EVER

Verse 3 says, "And there will no longer be a curse." Thank God, Genesis 3 will completely pass away and there will no longer be a curse. Everything introduced in Genesis 3 can be summed up in the word *curse*. Even death is a kind of curse. However, in the new heaven and new earth there will be no more curse, nor will there be any death. All of the history of sin will be over; man will glorify God well.

Verse 3 continues, "And the throne of God and of the Lamb will be in it." The situation here is unlike Genesis 3, where God walked in the garden in the cool of the day. Here God is reigning; His very throne is located here. Now the garden has become the city, the place where God is enthroned. "And His slaves will serve Him." What will the slaves of God do in eternity? They will serve Him. We should never think that in eternity we will have nothing to do. No, we will forever be His slaves, serving Him.

Verse 4 says, "And they will see His face, and His name will be on their forehead." All of our work for the Lord must be led by fellowship. True service to the Lord is in fellowship. Serving alone is not enough; there must be the fellowship. They will serve Him, and they will see His face. Oh, how many times when we see God we have already done His work. But I must say that we can do His work only after we see God. We should not be doing the work and constantly regretting—this is not fellowship. May God deliver us from any service which is not in fellowship, and may He save us from ever accomplishing any work without being able to fellowship after we have finished. We should never feel proud, self-content, or self-sufficient upon finishing the work. May God save us and deliver us from any kind of service which does not issue from fellowship and which is not in fellowship, and may He enable us to remain in fellowship even after we have finished the work. God's servants will not only have fellowship with Him, but "His name will be on their forehead." This is their testimony; this is what others who behold them will see. Everyone will know that these people are the people of God.

Verse 5 says, "And night will be no more; and they have no need of the light of a lamp and of the light of the sun, for the Lord God will shine upon them." In this city night is over. The lamp is the man-made light, and the sun is the natural light. All of man's work and all natural means will no longer be of any use because everything will be visible. Today we may be confused and not see clearly. Even after we have accomplished some service, we may not know where we are, but it will not be so in that day.

The last clause of verse 5 is the most important. "And they will reign forever and ever." This was the purpose of God in creation. In Genesis God's purpose was that man should rule, and now he has obtained that purpose—man is ruling. This is not something in the millennium. This passage of Scripture, Revelation 21 and 22, is not a description of the millennium, but of eternity. They will reign unto eternity, and they shall reign forever and ever. God's original goal is reached.

God wanted man to have dominion over the earth and to destroy Satan. Now man is reigning, and Satan has been cast into the lake of fire. God's purpose for the man He created has been attained. On the one hand, God wanted man to be like Himself, and on the other hand, God's appointed work for man was that he should rule. Now we have seen a bride—golden, glorious, and beautiful—with all kinds of treasure within her. She lacks nothing and is without spot, wrinkle, or any such things. Furthermore, she is holy and without blemish. She is truly clothed with glory. The glorious church spoken of in Ephesians 5 has been fulfilled in this way. What kind of work will those in the church do? They will reign forever and ever.

We may say that God's plan can be frustrated, but His plan can never be stopped. Since creation God's work has suffered much frustration. In fact, it seemed as if His work was being destroyed and that His plan would never succeed. But in Revelation God has reached His goal. There is a group of people full of pure gold, which is something of God. They are full of pearl, which is the work of Christ. And they are filled with precious stones, the work of the Holy Spirit. They will reign forever and ever.

Now that we have seen God's purpose and how He is working, what should we do? Should we hold a revival? Should we open a seminary? Or should we go back to our housework as usual? What are we doing here? God is doing a great thing. When we compare our work with His, how short we feel! May God be gracious to us, that having seen such a vision we will pay the full price. Once a man sees a vision he will be changed. May God give us a vision of what He is doing and what He is after. May He show us the kind of people He desires to obtain and how precious is that which He has set His heart upon. If we see these things, we will cry out and say, "Oh, how small I am! How much attention I have paid to myself!" And we will say, "If God does not work in me, I will never be able to do His work. Only when God Himself moves in me with His mighty power can I go on well." This great vision must overthrow us. It must cause us to see that our condition today can never satisfy God's heart. Our hope is that God would give us this vision. Once we have seen it, we will give our whole being to it; every part of us will be changed. Today we are standing between these two alternatives—being an overcomer or being a failure. How can any of us afford to be slack in prayer? If we neglect to pray, we will never be God's overcomer.

May the Lord Jesus, who has risen from the dead, that great Shepherd of the sheep, sustain us and lead us by His own mighty power that we may henceforth and forever belong to Him, forever consecrate to Him, forever serve Him, and forever go His way. May the Lord be gracious to us now and to eternity. Amen.

APPENDIX

THE OVERCOMERS AND
GOD'S DISPENSATIONAL MOVES

Scripture Reading: Rev. 12

According to the Bible, the seed of the woman will bruise the head of the enemy. The seed of the woman in Genesis 3 primarily refers to the Lord Jesus, but the overcomers also have a part in this seed. The seed of the woman includes the church, especially the overcomers. Even though the Lord bruised Satan's head, he is still at work. The fulfillment of the seed of the woman bruising Satan can be seen in the man-child in Revelation 12. The only Overcomer includes all the overcomers (vv. 10-11).

GOD DISPENSATIONAL MOVE—"NOW" (VERSE 10)

When God changes His attitude towards a certain matter, He makes a dispensational move. Every dispensational move brings in God's new way. His most important dispensational move is in Revelation 12. He wants to end this age and bring in the age of the kingdom. His purpose is not general and ordinary. How can He bring this age to a close and bring in another? He must have His dispensational instrument. This is what God wants to do today.

THE NEED OF THE MAN-CHILD

The rapture of the man-child brings an end to the church age and introduces the kingdom age. The man-child enables God to move. If there is not a man-child and a rapture, God cannot make a dispensational move. We should never forget that God can be limited. He waits for man in all of His moves. God's binding in heaven is based on our binding on earth;

God's loosing in heaven is based on our loosing on earth. Everything depends on the church.

It is God's desire that created beings would deal with fallen created beings. According to His purpose, the whole church should deal with Satan; however, the church has failed. Therefore, there is the need for the overcomers to rise up. God's purpose is fulfilled in the overcomers because they work with Him. We can see the principle of the overcomers throughout the Word of God. God always lays hold of a group of overcomers to make a dispensational move.

DISPENSATIONAL MOVES IN THE WORD OF GOD

After creation, life went on in a very ordinary way. Then God began with *Abraham*. God laid hold of Abraham and Sarah. He wanted a nation, but He began with just two people. God worked on these two, choosing them from out of all the other nations to produce a kingdom of priests. Abraham left his kindred and country. Abraham was greater than Abel, Enoch, and Noah because of God's choosing. It was as if these earlier men were quite ordinary. They had no dispensational value to God, but Abraham did. Then God said that his seed would go into Egypt and remain there for four hundred years. This was God's next move.

God laid hold of *Joseph,* not his brothers, and took him to Egypt. Joseph ruled in Egypt. God's actions were meant for good. Joseph was an overcomer in Egypt. He showed forth his power in the kingdom and showed forth his knowledge of God through dreams. God had made a dispensational move. He put an overcomer in Egypt; He did not put someone who could be defeated there. This is a principle of God's working.

After four hundred years, it was time for them to come out. At that point God laid hold of *Moses*. Without the events in the first few chapters of Exodus, there never would have been an exodus from Egypt. Moses came out of the water. He had an exodus from water. Then he had an exodus from Egypt. Moses was triumphant over death. God chose him to deal with Israel. Moses dwelt in the palace, which was the Egypt of Egypt. Not only did his spirit leave Egypt, but his body left Egypt as well; therefore, God chose him. Those who can only say, "Go," but not "Come," will have no effect. All of God's dispensational moves are based on one man. This is a principle of the overcomers.

When the nation of Israel wanted a king, the people chose Saul. He was a head taller than all the other men, but all of his ability was in his head. However, God chose His own king—*David.* Even when he was in the wilderness caring for the sheep, he was a king. He did not run when a lion came but went against it in the name of the Lord. Fear is not a kingly attitude, but when Goliath came, Saul was fearful. In contrast, David trusted in the Lord and went to fight against Goliath. Whoever is truly a king can be a king in any place. Later, David became a servant of Saul. When Saul became his enemy, David even had an opportunity to kill him, but he did not. Whoever cannot control himself is not worthy to be a king. There was no king of Israel greater than David. Only he was called King David, because he had dispensational value to God.

When Israel was taken into captivity for seventy years, God still had a dispensational move for Israel because of *Nehemiah;* he was a true overcomer. Even as he was serving a foreign king, he was preparing to go back to Jerusalem. He was not touched by Shushan and the affairs of the palace. Because God gained Nehemiah, He could make a dispensational move.

At the beginning of the New Testament, a group of special people were waiting in Jerusalem for the Lord Jesus. *Anna, Simeon,* and *all those* (Luke 2:38) were waiting for redemption in Israel. Their waiting brought in the fullness of the time, the Lord Jesus. God will not do things automatically; He will wait for His children to work with Him.

The Lord has two works on earth: redemption and building the church. The church is built on "this rock" (Matt. 16:18). The apostles were the first to stand on this rock. Even though they were weak in the flesh, their spirits were not weak. Because of this *the twelve apostles* have a special position— not even Paul is reckoned with them; they were a dispensational instrument. Paul said that he was less than the least of the apostles. The apostles and disciples waited for ten days, praying in Jerusalem. They might have said, "We have a great work to do after these days; we should rest now." Instead, they prayed. There were one hundred and twenty, but where were the others who had followed the Lord? Clearly, not everyone will work with God. These one hundred and twenty were overcomers.

DISPENSATIONAL MOVES IN CHURCH HISTORY

In church history the first special move was the *Reformation*. God used *Luther* in this dispensational move. The *Brethren* were also used. Darby, Groves, and Grant were His instruments. After the Welsh revival, a new move of God began. Both Evan Roberts and Mrs. Penn-Lewis knew about spiritual warfare; they knew how to deal with Satan. The truth of the kingdom began to be known in 1924. When Evan Roberts was seen after an absence of ten years, he said, "I have been praying kingdom prayers." Every time God wants to make a dispensational move, He must obtain His instrument.

Are we at the end of the age? If we are, the kingdom will soon begin. If a dispensational move is near, then God needs an instrument. General work is no longer adequate. The children of God lack a vision; they do not see the seriousness and intensity of the situation. *Now* is a matter of dispensation. Just being a good servant of the Lord is no longer good enough; this is not of great use to God. Please note that we are not saying that it is of no use. What are we doing to close this dispensation? What are we doing to bring in the next age? This is a special time, so there is the need of special Christians to do a special work.

Today God is waiting for the man-child. Only the rapture can precipitate the events in Revelation 12:10. God has an order, and He works according to that order. His eyes have left the church; they are now on the kingdom. An overcomer works according to the principle of the Body. The principle of the Body annuls sectarianism and individualism.

After the rapture the woman will be persecuted three and a half years. Many other of her children will go through the tribulation, but God will keep them. Being an overcomer is not primarily for escaping the tribulation. We need to see of what value the rapture is to the Lord, not to ourselves.

Of all the dispensational moves, the man-child is the greatest because it removes man's power and the devil's power, and it brings in the kingdom. We live in the most privileged time; we can do the most for God. *Light will show us the way, but strength and power will enable us to walk the road. A great price must be paid in order to be used now.*